Copyright © 2022 by Micah Allen Losh

All rights reserved.

No portion of this book may be reproduced in any form without written permission from the publisher or author, except as permitted by U.S. copyright law.

This memoir contains the "gangrenous speeches" of a "despicable," "mentally diseased," apostate. The locations, the names, and characteristics of those involved have been changed. Some events have been compressed or rearranged and some dialogue has been recreated.

Book Cover by Sara Riches.

Author Photo by Mica Renee and Tyler Robbins.

Mentally Diseased
Micah Allen Losh

Micah Allen Losh

Also by Micah Allen Losh

Gangrenous Speeches – Book Two in *The Apostasy Trilogy.*

Despicable – Book Three in *The Apostasy Trilogy.*

Sisu : Desolation before Motivation

Available on www.MicahAllenLosh.com

Dedicated to "Byrdie", who taught me the importance of spreading the truth.

Foreword

I met Micah Allen Losh when I was eighteen. I never truly knew who he was before and I never understood why I heard about him so much. I remember hearing things from "friends" I thought were both mine and his, but I was always baffled as to why he was so ostracized by people who claim to "promote the love of God." He was an "outcast," a "black sheep," and a "lost cause" in the eyes of many, but I never understood why. I believe I saw him for who he truly was, who nobody seemed to want to see him as. When I asked my parents and family, "Why don't you like him? You don't even know him. You know only of his reputation as a rebel," they told me to "cut ties with the ones who blatantly go against Jehovah's standards." I realized later that people didn't like him because he was brave. He had the courage to speak out and to push limits. I watched him be despised for struggling to fit into a world that seemed to hate him.

-ESG

Mentally Diseased
Micah Allen Losh

Micah Allen Losh

Awake

An oversimplification redundant with truth, certainly this is the fulcrum of salvation.
We are not a wretched brethren. No coven meant to covet sins.
Brothers and Sisters, alleged equality, Sisters and Brothers, elevated laity.
Huddle and circle as they circle the wagons.
The prize of perfection flaking away in deafening whispers passed through clenched teeth.
I am a vessel, too stained to be vestal. No matter the path it's banked by a devil.
Double back from an acrimonious path. Bleached with contrition. Fuck the past.
Obedience is obsequious. Mistaken masochism.
Know the horsemen are closing in. Witch hunts tarnish those judging sin.
Evil is abstract and long-term victimization can lead to defending the wicked.
These things are sick, I am sickened.
I am awake.

I scrawled forbidden thoughts, a violent expulsion of vitriol. The distinction between confidence and delusion drifted away as my certainty peeled off its mask to reveal confusion. Quietly, my reality ruptured, irrevocably fracturing my psyche. Some realizations are so earth-shattering that they bring about a birth and a death in the same moment — the simultaneous birth and death of the same person. My own cognitive dissonance had compounded to the point that I finally admitted something I could never admit — and this impossible admission brought forth countless more realizations I never wanted. An intrusive, ousted memory resurfaced, and reality got flimsier as it demanded to be remembered.

On a sweltering June day in Louisville, Kentucky Jesus called out to me.

"Hey little dude! Looking sharp." The cry came from a man dressed like Jesus.

My dress clothes exacerbated the oppressive heat. I really felt somewhat casual, since I had unbuttoned the top button of my shirt, loosened my tie, and rolled up my sleeves.

"Is Jesus a Jehovah's Witness?" I asked my parents, pointing at the man. "Is Jesus here for the District Convention?"

"No," my mother said. "That isn't Jesus — he's being sacrilegious. He's probably from the Grateful Dead concert next door."

"Oh." I had wondered if Jesus was going to be in the Sunday afternoon drama, which would be the only almost-enjoyable part of the three-day convention. Every year on the drive home, when they'd ask about my favorite part of the convention, I would surreptitiously say it was the drama.

"He's high on drugs. Drugs make you susceptible to demons," my mother explained.

"Yuck," I replied. I averted my eyes and made sure not to look at Jesus again. I certainly didn't want the demons inside of him to think *I* was interested in them.

As we moved toward the edge of the parking lot, I strained to hear a group of people I saw holding signs and yelling. My parents took note of this and warned me to not even look in their direction, much less read their signs or listen to them, because they were apostates who served Satan. I started singing to Jehovah to make sure I couldn't hear the apostates and to fight off their demonic influence. I resented the apostates' very presence, and then I smirked while I relished a vision of Jehovah slaughtering them at Armageddon. I'll never be an apostate, I thought.

I'm an apostate, I thought, as I reallocated myself in my body. A new, suffocating comprehension rewrote my past, unraveled my future and rotted the foundation of my very existence.

I gagged on the absurdity of the four Armageddon go-bags my mother had meticulously packed and placed in the family coat closet for us. An unrecognizable clamor startled me out of my befuddled haze. What began as laughter crystallized as sorrow when it met the air, coming from me without effort or intention. I was on the precipice of a personal cataclysm. I would like to tell you I avoided the worst of it, but that would be a lie and I was raised to spread the "truth." I chugged a beer, brushed my teeth and headed back to work as tears cascaded from my eyes — eyes that had been faithfully on the prize of immortality for 37 years.

Christian Youth

Take my life.
Christ!
I've bled, been drained of love.
Blood!
Born in the midst of sin and told to live a wish.
There's not an antidote, just proverbs you can quote.
We're in this for the end.
We're your only friends.
We'll take you to the end.
We have to be with you so you don't deviate.
We'll always be with you, our prayers are all for you.
You'll always be with us, we will leave all of them.
What do you say my friend?
We'll take you to the end!

My mother began reading Jehovah's Witness publications aloud to me while I was still in utero. The lifestyle I would be born into was unbelievably demanding physically, mentally, and emotionally. I would be cut off from the world of nonbelievers, and my days would be built around never-ending prayer, study, meetings, and preaching.

I was molded into an unwitting, obedient, circumscribed version of myself that championed an ideology I never questioned. I was told I was the recipient of "undeserved kindness," and that I was a "good-for-nothing-slave," and I believed it.

From boyhood, I spoke of prophecy. I heralded destruction. I lived with the expectation of a perfect life on a paradise Earth. I knew that when it came, I'd grow young again, greet the resurrected dead, befriend every animal without fear, master every hobby, learn every instrument, build countless houses, and watch my family line extend forever.

I don't have many memories from my childhood, and that may be because it wasn't worth remembering. Maybe the years of religious monotony and miserable school days bled together into a forgettable blur.

The life I'd been born into exhausted me on every level. Daily, I read from the Bible as well as from a devotional, meditated, prayed before each meal, and I was ready to informally preach at any moment. Weekly, I had a night of personal study, a night of family worship, and three congregational meetings to attend. Before each of these meetings, I had study material to read and I needed to prepare myself to answer questions or read from scripture. I had to arrive early for meetings, then stay late to "encourage others," sing songs, audibly say "Amen" again and again, and clean the building. I was expected to preach at least once a week. I'd keep records of my householders, the literature I'd placed with them, and any donations I'd received. Every month there would be new magazines I had to read, and I'd be required to turn in records from at least ten hours of preaching and field service. Annually, we held a remembrance of Christ's death, two one-day circuit assemblies, and a three-day regional convention. If someone's job wouldn't allow them to take time off to attend all three days of the convention, that person would be advised to quit.

As I endeavored to maintain a good reputation with my congregation and to curry enough favor with Jehovah to gain eternal life, my exhaustion compounded. I saw countless people forget about their hobbies, avoid higher education, work dead-end jobs, repress their sexualities and remain single and childless – they were putting their whole *lives* on the back burner so that they could prioritize their spirituality.

My obedience was rooted in a fear made concrete by a book called *Revelation*, which was filled with pulpy, apocalyptic illustrations sandwiched between red covers that reminded me of blood. I always thought the book was rather convoluted, even before I had the words to describe it. However, after a Sister in the congregation told me that Armageddon would probably come before I finished high school, I found myself frequently examining the pictures. Every night, after I prayed to Jehovah and asked Him to destroy all nonbelievers, I'd lie in bed with my eyes wide open. I didn't want to close them and see the horsemen of the apocalypse, famine, fire raining down from heaven, the streets turned to rivers of blood, and the birds of heaven feasting on the bodies of the dead. I was taught that Jehovah could read my mind and my heart. I hoped He wouldn't kill me for being afraid of Him.

When I started kindergarten, I expected to be hated because I was no part of the world. I was scared, but I was also emboldened in my knowledge that I served the one true God, and I had already been preaching door-to-door for years. Our evangelist efforts were sometimes called "spiritual warfare," but we were never violent, even when householders shouted us down and threatened violence. Vengeance belonged to Jehovah, and I was supposed to rejoice in being mistreated and "to turn the other cheek." I didn't expect Jehovah to protect me. Jehovah hadn't protected Jesus, and there were many other loyal Christians He chose not to protect. Even at Armageddon – *especially* at Armageddon – survival wasn't guaranteed.

School was a unique territory that Jehovah's Witnesses could only infiltrate through their children. Weeks before I started class, my mother thoroughly prepared me to answer every question I could be asked, to introduce myself in a Christian way, and to preach whenever the opportunity arose. We rehearsed and rehearsed – there was a lot of memorization. I was good at it. When I met my first teacher, I was ready.

"Hi. My name is Micah and I'm one of Jehovah's Witnesses. I'd like to give you a brochure that explains my beliefs."

"Hello, Micah," Ms. Simms said cheerfully. "I'd be glad to take that brochure from you." She accepted the brochure under the guise of it being an informational resource. It was disingenuous of me, but this was life-saving work.

"Have you ever had a Jehovah's Witness student before?" I asked.

"A few. You don't believe in medicine, right?"

"We go to the doctor and take medicine, but we don't accept blood transfusions."

"Well, what if you need a blood transfusion to save your life?"

"I would die," I said, without any understanding of death. "Blood transfusions aren't guaranteed to work anyway. The Bible says to abstain from blood, so I won't eat food with blood in it either. If I die loyal to Jehovah, He can give me eternal life."

"Okay. Anything else I need to know?"

"I don't celebrate birthdays, holidays, salute the flag, say the Pledge of Allegiance or believe in evolution. If we have assignment related to any of those things, I would like to ask to please do an alternative assignment."

"Okay, Micah. I'm looking forward to being your kindergarten teacher!"

I didn't want to go to school, and I certainly didn't want to preach to my classmates, but I had no choice. When an opportunity to preach presented itself, I'd worry that if I didn't take the chance, I'd be blood-guilty, and Jehovah would kill me at Armageddon.

Once school began, I steadfastly rejected my classmates' kindness, holiday greetings, birthday wishes, and any food or gifts that accompanied them. When they'd hold parties, I would sit in the hall and eat the snacks my mother had packed for me. I hated school, but my parents told me it was necessary preparation for getting a job. I wanted to go unnoticed, but people – especially children – are curious when you choose to be an outcast.

Again and again, I explained to my classmates the ways my life was different from theirs. I couldn't shop at or attend any store or event with ties to false religions, I couldn't own a cross, I couldn't throw rice at weddings, dance suggestively, vote, say "God bless you," be entertained by magic, read horoscopes, do yoga, practice martial arts, go skydiving, or follow trends. Beyond the rigid rules of my faith, there were many "conscience matters" which fell to the discretion of my parents. I couldn't participate in any extracurricular activities at school, eat Lucky Charms, eat food associated with pagans, eat candy cigarettes, wear band t-shirts or clothing with skulls, and there was a limit on how much black clothing I could own. I couldn't have toy guns, but squirt guns were okay. I was warned against buying secondhand items, watching horror movies, listening to heavy metal, and playing role-playing games, because they all could invite demons into my life.

Telling my classmates and teachers that they were disobeying Jehovah and that He would kill them if they refused to repent made me about as popular as you would expect. I was horrified to learn that so many of my classmates were being fed lies about things like Santa and the Easter Bunny. Satan told the first lie; lying was *imitating* Satan.

One morning, in second grade, a classmate came running up to me, brimming with excitement.

"The stork brought me a new baby brother!"

"Your parents are liars. They had sex." It was severe, but I felt entitled – and *compelled* – to speak to her that way, because I knew the truth.

Mistreatment seemed to be the natural reward for following Jehovah. At the time that I was facing these trials, my faith was my shield and comfort. It never occurred to me until later this same shield and comfort might be the very cause of my acting in such a way as to invite mistreatment upon myself. When my second-grade teacher refused to let me out of the locked classroom to use the bathroom, I began fervently praying to my God. I shit in my pants. I continued to pray as I tied my jacket around my waist, awkwardly walked to the school bus and made my way to a seat. After an interminable and jarring ride home, I collapsed in front of my mother tearfully. She seemed disinterested in my plight – or maybe she was proud under the surface. She told me I was no part of the world and that

Jesus always said we'd be persecuted. My persecution wasn't as bad as those of others – I decided I'd rather shit my pants than be eaten by lions.

I only remember a few minutes from May 18, 1996. My friend Saul and I were tossing a ball back and forth in the basement of my childhood home when I heard what I thought was a siren. I realized what it was when it faltered and returned, a woman shrieking. I also realized what it meant. My father was dead. Over the past year, I had watched the chemotherapy devour my father as if it preferred him to the kidney cancer. I wasted time praying while my father wasted away.

Members of our congregation lined the hallway approaching my parents' – now just my mother's – bedroom. My mother's howling didn't stop or falter as I opened the door to her room, her living grief starkly contrasted with my father's slack, lifeless body. My father was not the only one that died that day.

My father was a rarity, because his viewing and service were in a funeral parlor. I don't know exactly why we broke tradition for him; most funerals were held in the Kingdom Hall with no body or urn. No one seemed to take issue with the unconventional service, though. We made our way to our seats as a brother from Bethel sang a song about paradise. I would never again be able to hear that song without being transported back into my thirteen-year-old body. My fantasies about swimming with great white sharks transfigured into fantasies of seeing my dead father after he was resurrected. My father's own life was a footnote in his funeral, a subservient illustration that might assist the true believers in the great commission of winning souls.

"That was a bunch of bullshit." My uncle Benedict stood with me and the rest of my father's side of the family for the song following the service. They dispersed as Brother Lakstins sauntered over.

"Be *proud* your dad died loyal to Jehovah!" Brother Lakstins' voice always boomed, but the joyful note in his oration only served to deepen my sense of loss and confusion over how to feel about it. "He will be resurrected, and you need to be there to see him." He clapped my shoulder and smiled me.

"I am," I said, looking at the coffin holding my father's husk. I didn't feel pride. I felt sadness and anger. Jehovah could have saved my father and he didn't. Even as an act of omission, I hated Jehovah for my father's death, and further hated myself for hating

Jehovah. My father was dead, he looked dead, he felt dead to my touch. I wanted him back.

I didn't allow myself to grieve my father, because I couldn't. What justification is there for grief, when his pain has ended, and resurrection is dangled before you like a carrot? I went on with the only life I knew, trying and failing to be a better Jehovah's Witness. Less than four months after I bore my father's coffin to the grave, and almost twelve years before my prefrontal cortex was fully developed, I was baptized and dedicated my life to Jehovah God. My father's death was really the only reason I went through the process. I just wanted the chance to see him again. My memories of it never really stood out to me. I only know the exact date – September 7, 1996 – because my mother gave me a bracelet to commemorate it.

Bad Association

Within despair, among decadence and before a promised embrace.
Distractions are burdens as I await his forgotten face.
If angels fall are demons redeemed? There are cracks in the armor of your Holy regime.
Certainly, once you've gone so far return is a betrayal of self.
There are limits to what I can disbelieve.
The faithful devout are devoured by doubt.
The truth like blood waits to get out.
Apathy for the dogma.
Antipathy for the devotee.
Bliss lies in ignorance, are you lying to me?
If death won't have me perhaps sleep will, contentment in cycles but none of it real.

Lucas was the only friend that tolerated my prolonged heartache. We got drunk in his basement when I was thirteen. Things spiraled from there: we picked up vandalism, running into garage doors at night, squirting shampoo on windows, leaving bologna on cars, putting food coloring in pools, taping pornography onto porches, yelling "Butt sex!" at random people in traffic, and even staged a child abduction with Lucas' younger brother, Cliff.

One Tuesday night, I stashed a baseball bat and a metal rod in my trunk and Lucas and I told our parents we were going for ice cream.

POP! "Fuck you!" The roar of the engine, the wind in my ears, the satisfying pop of each felled mailbox, and our own shouted swears swirled together into a cacophony of frenzied destruction. Turning around in the cul-de-sac, we saw a single untouched mailbox left standing. I pulled back up to it and Lucas hopped out and beat it into a crumple. Reveling in the excitement for a moment, we decided to switch places when I spotted a parked SUV that seemed suspicious. They had been idling for a minute without moving. I didn't know what to do – and I wasn't really *thinking* either – so for reasons I could never explain, I hit the suspicious vehicle's window, hard.

To my surprise, the window shattered, and I heard someone shouting our location. I yelled to Lucas to drive away from the scene, but the white SUV followed us closely. Lucas pulled over and we switched places – I didn't want him to get charged with driving while underage on top of everything else we'd done that night. I ran red lights and stop signs, but I couldn't lose the white SUV. He followed us with such intensity that I was almost relieved when I saw the red and blue lights in my rearview mirror. Lucas and I were handcuffed, loaded into the squad car, and delivered to a juvenile detention center, where we were put into holding cells. I was relieved when my mother and Lucas' parents arrived, until I saw their faces. My mother didn't say a word to me until we were home.

"After book study you vandalized people! You broke the law!" my mother yelled.

"I wasn't thinking," I said.

"Lucas' dad was driving around looking in ditches for you two!"

"I don't know why I did it." I didn't know what to do with this anger.

"I was telling the officer that you were good boys who served Jehovah when we found out you'd been arrested!"

"Mom, I'm sorry," I said as I stifled laughter.

"It's not funny!"

"I know."

"Go to bed. You're probably going to have to talk to the elders."

"Why?"

"Because you represent Jehovah! People in the community know that you're a Witness!"

I wanted my mother to talk to me about loss. I wanted to know how she handled her mother's death when she was five. That conversation never came; maybe my mother didn't know how to have it.

When Lucas and I walked into a room filled with the people whose property we'd vandalized, their collective anger was palpable. Everyone went around the room and talked about what had been going through their heads that night. There was an elderly couple present who spoke last. Their mailbox was the one that we had missed and come back for. They told us about how they were afraid we were in a gang and would retaliate against them, how their grandson had joined a gang and died. Lucas and I both burst into tears – we never meant to frighten people, least of all a frail, elderly couple. After everyone had spoken, the couple hugged us and told us we were good boys who had just made a mistake. I felt relieved and hopeful after they forgave us. If worldly people were so generous and forgiving, surely the elders would be even more so.

"Dear heavenly father Jehovah, we ask that you influence our decision tonight," Brother Reed prayed. "We ask that you help us to reach Micah's heart and to make him realize the severity of his actions." Brother Reed was talking about me to God. I was enthralled. I knew Jehovah's Holy Spirit must have been in the room with us, but I couldn't seem to sense it.

"Do you understand the consequences of your actions?" Brother Martin asked sternly.

"I broke the law," I said. "I scared people and damaged their property. It was wrong and I'll never do it again."

"It's more serious than that."

"Oh." I was a little surprised.

"While that is the correct attitude, you need to consider the ramifications of what you've done," Brother Reed said.

"I know I made a mistake," I said quietly. "I wasn't thinking."

"You need to think *seriously* about the people whose property you destroyed and the police officers that arrested you," said Brother Martin.

"Think about what?" I was frightened by his tone.

"You made a dedication to Jehovah, didn't you?"

"Yes."

"You promised to obey Jehovah and part of obeying Him is submitting to the secular authorities that He has allowed to be in place."

"Oh," I replied in a shameful whisper. "I don't know why I did it." *I'm so fucking stupid.*

"You've brought reproach on yourself, your parents, and most importantly, your heavenly father," Brother Reed said. "What if people in the community reject our message because of your actions?"

"I don't know." *Would someone really reject the true religion just because I hit mailboxes?*

"You would be blood-guilty! Do you understand what that means, son?" I could tell Brother Reed was earnestly upset – the force of his words sprayed saliva my way. I winced.

"Yes." I hated him for calling me son.

"If Jehovah found you blood-guilty, you would be *destroyed* and miss out on eternal life!"

"I know."

"What about Lucas? You've endangered his life as well. You're older, you're supposed to be someone he can look up to."

"I'm sorry," I said, and I meant it. *Please, please don't disfellowship me.*

Neither brother Reed nor brother Martin had asked me how I was doing since my dad had died. You'd imagine that men with children of their own would be able to sympathize and remember that teenagers are often stupid and thoughtless, but their only concern was how my actions reflected on the congregation and Jehovah. As I laid in bed that night, I imagined sitting before Jehovah on judgement day and Him telling me I had to die because I hit mailboxes when I was sixteen. I was terrified.

On a Thursday night, Lucas and I were publicly reproved in an announcement to the Cragwell congregation. A Sister in the hall burst into tears at the announcement. I was told that public reproof was an attempt to reach my heart and help me to hate my actions and repent, but I didn't need to cultivate hatred for vandalism because I didn't love vandalism. Instead, I cultivated hatred for myself. There was a 'local needs talk' about being a positive representative for Jehovah in the community, which culminated in Lucas' father being forced to step down from eldership and my mother and I no longer being allowed to host book-study. Lucas and I each lost our "privileges" to comment, read scripture, and run microphones during meetings. I was assigned an older elder, Brother Meyers, as a study partner. He wanted me to learn the books of the Bible forwards and backwards. Ironically, I was still allowed to go door-to-door and preach in the same neighborhoods I had terrorized and been arrested in.

Our punishment was multifaceted. Lucas and I were kept apart for the summer. We paid restitution to our victims, I had to sell all my video games and my console, and I had to tell the people at the second-hand store why I was selling it. My mother would time my drive to work and back, and if I went over time, I'd have to sell my car. If I wasn't at school or my job, I had to go wherever my mother went. Lucas and I were both required to participate in a diversion program for first-time underage offenders.

What made me repent wasn't the punishments doled out by the elders or my mother, and it wasn't the shame of public reproof either. It was when Lucas and I had met with the people we vandalized, when our victims shared more acceptance and forgiveness with us than I had ever found among Jehovah's Witnesses. It affected me deeply, but at the same time, another part of me dismissed them. I wasn't raised to empathize with nonbelievers, so I tried to convince myself that I repented for some other reason.

I had attended Cragwell congregation for sixteen years. My parents and I had helped build the Kingdom Hall, my father had attended his last meeting there, but a rift had been growing since he died. My public reproof certainly hadn't helped. Most of the congregation avoided me, but some went as far as belittling me for being depressed. One Brother told me that I needed to get over my dad, that I had been too sad for too long. A Sister told me that my mother's loss was greater than mine. I was told to pray and read the Bible to combat the grief, but it never worked. I interpreted it as evidence of my own sin.

"I don't want to be alive," I told my mother. It wasn't easy to say it out loud.

"I'll ask the elders to talk to you," my mother replied. I had hoped *she* would talk to me, especially about her experience with losing her mother.

The elders wouldn't talk to me; instead, they told my mother that I was just "looking for attention." It felt like a personal rejection from God.

"Why won't the elders meet with me?" I asked.

"I don't know. We're going to switch congregations."

When I was eighteen, I packed a bag and was admitted into a stress center – the switch to Paleland congregation hadn't helped. The glass doors of the locked unit hissed open and stale air enveloped me. I went to the group therapy sessions and met with my therapist, but there was a disconnect between my words and my emotions. I went through an inkblot test and was told it was inconclusive. I kept telling my therapist I wanted to die, and she just kept asking why. I couldn't bear to tell them it was because Jehovah had rejected me through his elders. I couldn't possibly explain to them that despite being born into the true religion, I wasn't happy, that I feared I was wicked beyond redemption, because I knew how crazy I would sound.

I felt guilty for being around "worldly" people, so I tried to isolate myself as much as I could. Most of the techs were unpleasant, and the only place they didn't frequent was the smoking area, so I spent as much time as I could there. Smoking honestly seemed even more taboo than hitting mailboxes – I knew people that had been disfellowshipped *just* for smoking.

While I was there once, a morbidly obese woman seated across from me held out her cigarettes.

"You want one of these?" As she spoke, I followed the crisscrossing lacerations on her arm – fresh wounds overlapping old scars – up to meet her eyes, which were surrounded by bruises.

"Sure. You got a light?"

"I got you, sugar." She winked as she lit the cigarette and handed it to me. I tried not to grimace at her infected eyebrow piercing. "Fuck, boy, what're *you* doing in here?"

"Um..." I took a drag, repulsed by the taste but enamored with the sense of rebellion. "I just want to die," I said softly.

"Why'd you wanna go and do that, huh? You gotta have *fun*!" She started swaying around and snapping her fingers in some kind of rhythm in what seemed like an approximation of dancing, her cigarette flapping around her toothless mouth.

"Yeah." *You're in here too.*

"I don't give a fuck! I'm so fucking horny right now, I'll take dick *or* pussy!" She beamed at me, eyes twinkling.

"Oh." I didn't know how to respond, but I knew I definitely didn't want any more information.

"I might just take that long ashtray and fuck it! Suck it clean by morning! I don't give a ***fuck***!" At this point, she was screaming with a ferocity reserved exclusively for the unhinged.

"Cleanliness is next to Godliness," I said, really to myself, as techs stormed the room. I escaped to my room, but I could still hear them strapping her down and struggling in vain to calm her. She called them bitches and kept asking if they were gonna fuck her. She was still screaming her head off when I met with my therapist that afternoon.

"Will you tell me about your friends?" Dr. Muller asked in her thick German accent.

"James, Ozzy, Trent, Marilyn, Maynard, Till."

"How often do you spend time with them?"

"Every day," I said softly. Then I felt guilty for lying to her. "Those are actually just my favorite singers."

"Do you not have any friends, Micah?"

"Well, a lot of Jehovah's Witnesses get married at 18, and the couples tend to avoid single people. All of my friends are married or engaged, I mean, one couple even got engaged at 15. And a lot of people have distanced themselves from me since my dad died."

"Have you ever thought about leaving the Jehovah's Witnesses?"

"Why would I do that?" I asked. *How could I do that?*

"By your own admission, you're excluded."

"I am."

"It doesn't sound like you're happy."

"Yeah."

"Let me be honest with you: unless you're hiding some dark secret, I don't believe there is anything wrong with you. There is no reason you couldn't get a girlfriend, go to college, meet people, and have a life."

"Okay." I couldn't really entertain the idea of leaving. If I left, I'd lose my mom and never see my dad again.

"It's just something to consider."

Dr. Muller wasn't wrong – while friendship with other Jehovah's Witnesses was compulsory, the onus was on you to socialize, and no one was meeting me halfway. I would hear fanciful stories of love, kindness, and acceptance, and when I couldn't make those things happen in my own life, I just prayed.

The week I turned 21, I died. I carefully laid out five rows of blue and white sleeping pills, taking a grim, moribund glee in alternating the colors. I choked the pills down and looked at the corpulent, makeup caked woman on my television. *You're going to die a virgin, and she's the last woman you'll ever look at.* These were the last words I remember thinking as I closed my eyes and waited for sleep. Death was coming, and I didn't want to be awake for it.

"What's wrong with you? Did you take something?" My mother's shrill, concerned voice brought me back to some semblance of reality. I realized that I too was bellowing, yelling so loudly that the vibrations and exertion had shaken me out of bed. I found myself slumped against the wall, my bedroom door flung open. Evidently there was a part of me that didn't want to die.

"Something." I reflexively convulsed as my dog sniffed my hand. With my other hand, I feebly gestured towards my room. Words were difficult to come across, and my eyes felt so heavy. Intending to close my eyes for only a moment, I opened them to find paramedics kneeling beside me. *This is it. I'll either sleep forever or wake up in paradise.* I closed my eyes for the last time and waited for the coming oblivion.

Disfellowshipping

I am a pariah among the chosen, the chosen ones...oh yes!
But never mind.
You aren't one of us and I shouldn't even be talking to you about this.
Promised eternity and given nothing, always promised.
Constantly reassured and caressed and the blinding hypocrisy is making my teeth grind.
Grinding into crumbling into mumbling. No murmuring.
I'm just prey. I won't pray.
Pleas and pleading will not sate the needing.
I am not in the fold despite what I'm told.
Surrounded yet alone. I fear the unknown.
I cannot exist and it's death to resist.

I woke up in hell. Unable to move, unable to speak, suffocating and starving, my screams muffled by an obstruction that ran from mouth to stomach –

"Knock-knock!" A cheery singsong voice announced the arrival of a nurse. I was in a hospital. Unable to respond, she continued without missing a beat. "Honey, you've been in a coma for 37 hours." She didn't seem surprised to find me awake. I was quiet as she removed the restraints, ventilator, feeding tube and catheter. She quietly mused to herself as she worked, like a mother over an infant. "You're sure lucky, you must have had an angel looking out for you!"

"I really doubt it." My voice sounded foreign to me after the ordeal.

"I don't think God's finished with you yet."

"Maybe." *God was finished with my father.*

I came out of the hospital unscathed. Numerous doctors and nurses told me that this was evidence that God didn't want my life to be over yet. I disagreed then and I disagree now. I was in facilities for two weeks and when I got out, I was told that my mother had asked the elders to announce what had happened. Two people visited me out of the hundreds that were notified or heard about it second-hand.

"Jehovah makes things known" was a common saying among Jehovah's Witnesses. Growing up as a Jehovah's Witness inures one to having their own emotions weaponized against themselves and doing the same unto others. This weaponization – this tattletale culture – comes in many forms: mostly subtle (and not so subtle) social cues, but most notably in the punishment of disfellowshipping. Only a baptized Jehovah's Witness can be disfellowshipped – a process severing social, spiritual, and even familial bonds. It was life and death: hiding your "sin" or the "sin" of another meant that Jehovah would withdraw His spirit from the entire congregation.

Life in the congregation since my father's death had been volatile and lonely, so I was very excited at the prospect of a childhood friend, Jessica, joining the Paleland congregation. I was twenty-three years old and I hadn't seen Jessica since we were kids. She was a few years older than me, and, truth be told, I'd always had a little crush on her – though I never let that affect our friendship.

We reconnected and ended up spending a lot of time together until we found ourselves at a concert – just the two of us. Other Jehovah's Witnesses continually asked us if we were dating, since if you're not related, spending that much time with the opposite sex *is* dating. I always brushed them off, but I found myself silently wondering about it when we arrived at the concert. We got drunk in the car before heading inside.

"If you want more to drink, I could always just flash somebody." Jessica offered it glibly, like she was just suggesting we ask a stranger for directions in a new town.

"No, you don't have to do that."

"Come on, I will, it's not a big deal."

"I don't want you to do that." I hadn't seen this side of Jessica before. I didn't like it – it almost frightened me.

"I'm just a whore anyway." She said it with a dismissive, throwaway attitude, but I could tell that she was speaking from the heart. She believed what she was saying.

"Not to me. You shouldn't talk about yourself like that – you're more than that to me."

Jessica kissed me. She was the first woman I'd ever kissed. She climbed on top of me in my seat, which got us kicked out of the concert, but we didn't mind. As I leaned against her car with her head in my lap, all I could think about was how lovely she looked.

"I don't think either of us should drive home," Jessica said as she reached up to touch my face. "I'll call my boyfriend to come pick us up."

"Your boyfriend?" I asked. *What the fuck?*

"I've told him all about you. How we've been friends since we were kids."

"That's great," I said flatly as I pushed her hand away.

"What happened?" Jessica asked me the next morning.

"We kissed."

"I'm so sorry! It doesn't change anything between us." There was little pause between her responses. She sounded canned.

"Okay," I said, but I didn't think it was true. "How long have you been with your boyfriend?"

"Months. I'm really trying to not have sex."

"You know I'm obligated to tell the elders."

Jessica didn't respond. She silently acquiesced to the nature of things. Brother Buchard, the elder assigned to counsel me seemed far more concerned with punishing Jessica than me. I should have been counseled for being alone and unchaperoned with Jessica, but I wasn't. Brother Buchard reassured me that I was doing the loving thing, but his words rang hollow in face of my guilt.

After he left, I felt drained, empty, alone. I gulped down handfuls of pills with vodka.

I don't remember how I got to the hospital, but I do remember the sorrow in Jessica's eyes when she came to see me.

"What do you want?" Jessica asked.

I want you. "It doesn't matter," I said.

The night Jessica was disfellowshipped – it wasn't her first time – I stayed home and got drunk. Going for an aimless walk, I called Jessica, not sure whether I even wanted her to pick up or not. Straight to voicemail. It hurt to be rejected, especially by Jessica. Not only me, she had rejected Jehovah, eternal life, and the fellowship of the only system of social "support" we knew. I was livid. I felt terribly guilty. I was ashamed of my own sinful impulses, ashamed of feeling led on by Jessica. All of this was swirling in my drunken mind until I heard the recording beep, triggering a torrent of half-understood, half-expressed emotions. I screamed at one of my dearest friends to enjoy being a whore, that her being a whore was why her father had to leave her mother and sisters and start another family. I unleashed everything that had built up over months, years, I didn't even know how long, until I felt empty. After I hung up, the empty numbness was replaced with quiet guilt. I couldn't bring myself to apologize, since I was supposed to be shunning her. Funny how that didn't stop my previous message. I couldn't admit it at the time, but I resented Jehovah Himself and my "duty" to police His congregation.

A few months after Jessica was disfellowshipped, a woman named Kim moved from Benjamin congregation to Paleland. We started spending a lot of time together, and I planned a proposal for our one year anniversary. In our eleventh month of dating we went to a concert in Ohio with our friend Matthew chaperoning us. I didn't realize anything was amiss until we were merging onto the interstate.

"Mother*fucker*!" Kim screamed as she swerved her car towards a mini-van, chasing it off the on-ramp and into the grass. Inside the car, a child's hands pressed against the window. "That little shit gave me a dirty look!"

I stared at her with disbelief. Matthew gave no response. This crazy bitch did it on purpose.

"Have you been drinking?" I asked, surprised at how calm I sounded.

"I took some Vicodin and Xanax earlier. My cramps have been really bad." Kim floored it and started laughing hysterically. We sped toward a semi-trailer with a pyramid of logs strapped to the bed and just barely missed the trailer on my side. *I'm 23 and I've never done anything.* Kim took her eyes off the road to rifle through her purse, so I reached out to steady the wheel. *Where the fuck are the cops?*

"I've got it!" Kim shouted as she slapped my hand. "I need directions." Kim's phone was already dialing the assistance number – what we used before we had GPS – when she put it on speaker. The Middle Eastern woman on the line struggled to understand Kim's slurring. "Learn how to speak English! Get out of my country!" Kim shrieked as she grabbed the wheel. I looked in the backseat and Matthew had a road map over his face.

I'm going to die today, in this car, with this crazy asshole. Somehow, we made it to Ohio and Kim pulled into a gas station. She went inside.

"What the fuck?" I turned toward the backseat to look at Matthew. "We *cannot* let her drive anymore."

"We made it to Ohio, we're almost there." His lack of concern amazed me.

"We can't just die today." I spotted Kim coming back towards the car. "Hey, did you want me to drive?"

"No," Kim snapped.

"Are you sure? You seem tired." *You seem drunk.*

"Come on!"

"Look, I don't feel comfortable getting back into the car with you."

"Why?"

"Your driving frightened me, we nearly wrecked numerous times."

"No I didn't."

"I'm not getting back in the car. You say you just took some pills but you're obviously trashed."

"You call me trash? I can drink if I want!"

"You're too messed up to even hear me!"

"Fine! You two bitches stay here." Kim got back in the car and pulled away, leaving me and Matthew stranded a state away from home.

After the concert ended, Kim called and offered to pick us up. I told her curtly not to worry about me or how I got home. My mother was already on her way to Ohio to pick up Matthew and me. The next morning, my cellphone and home phone alternated ringing. Speaking to Kim was near the last thing I wanted to do, but I eventually answered.

"Hello?" I put as much of an edge into my greeting as I could muster.

"Micah? Are you – I mean, how are you?"

"Fine." It felt good to be curt with Kim after what she put Matthew and me through.

"Listen, I just wanted to say that I'm so sorry, my cramps were just driving me crazy and I didn't know how – "

"You could have killed us. All of us. You were acting crazy, and I don't know if I want anything more to do with that."

"Please! Micah, you know how much I love you. I swear, nothing like this will ever happen again."

I hesitated. On some level, I knew that she was just saying whatever it took to move past the incident. But I did feel love for her in that moment, as painful as it might have been. I accepted her apology and decided to take her back, on the condition that she stop drinking. She readily agreed.

Just two Sundays later, I could smell the booze on her as we sang the opening song before meeting. Kim held my hand while we bowed our heads to pray; I squeezed her hand and she squeezed mine back. I knew I had to break up with her.

On an emotional level, it was hard. But the words came more easily than I expected. She seemed okay enough with parting ways.

After the breakup, I was once again tormented by lingering feelings of guilt. Certain phrases, Bible quotations, elder exhortations spoke specifically, as though they were direct signs of Jehovah prompting me to confess, to repair my relationship with Him. I confessed my sins in prayer and supplicated Jehovah to forgive me, but it never felt like enough. I contacted the elders and told them I needed to discuss some wrongdoing.

The back room of the Kingdom Hall was stuffy. Little air moved around there. When the lights were on, a harsh fluorescent buzzing supported the words of the elders, a discordant accompaniment that mocked the old associations between music and the spirit.

"I stayed overnight with Kim. It was just the two of us, we were alone, drinking and we kissed." I confessed succinctly. Brothers Froyer and Vivitier listened with polite interest. I hoped my brief synopsis would suffice.

"How many times did this happen?" Brother Vivitier inquired. "Did your contact ever go any further than kissing?"

"It happened a few times." I mumbled. "Her bra did come off." Brother Froyer scrawled in his notebook as I spoke.

"Kim exposed her breasts? Did you touch them?"

"Yes." *Please stop asking me questions.*

"How did you touch her breasts?"

"What do you mean?" I hated the way he kept saying breasts.

"What I mean is, with what part of your body did you touch them?"

"Hands, mouth." My words were robotic and sounded distant in my ears.

"Did you become aroused?"

"Yes." My hands over my face muffled the word.

"Did you touch each other's genitals?"

"No."

"There was no sexual intercourse?"

"No."

"You didn't have a sexual release?"

"No." *I already told you what happened.*

"You two slept in the same bed and there was no immorality?" Brother Froyer asked suspiciously.

"Yeah." I said. *I brought this to you.*

"Is there anything else you'd like to tell us?" Brother Froyer smiled at me as he placed his hands neatly on the notebook he'd been writing in.

"No." I wanted to get as far away from them as I possibly could. Rather than the relief I expected to feel when unburdening myself of my sins, I was mortified.

"We want to commend you for your honesty and for bringing this matter to the elders." Brother Viviter said. "We'll speak with Kim sometime this week and get back with you."

Next week, I found myself in a judicial committee. Brothers Froyer and Viviter were there, but the meeting was led by Brother Slice.

"We'd like to begin by asking for Jehovah's blessing." Brother Slice carefully over-enunciated "Jehovah" as he spoke. They briefly recapitulated what I had already told the elders in the last meeting, which Brother Slice had surely already read from Brother Froyer's notes. Afterwards, I was dismissed to the auditorium.

A disfellowshiping means many things, but the only one on my mind was the separation from Jehovah. He would take His Holy Spirit away from me. His precious mediator, the Holy Spirit, whom I imagined filling the back room and guiding the elders' decision as they intervened on my behalf. I prayed to Jehovah for what I feared would be the last time He would hear me.

"We're ready for you," Brother Viviter said. I started feeling icy all throughout my body, I followed him to the back room and sat down.

"We have decided to proceed with a disfellowshipping." Brother Slice announced this perfunctorily, like he was announcing a change in a train departure time.

"Oh." *Had Jehovah read my heart? Had he deemed me unrepentant?*

"What we struggle to understand is what could have stopped a red-blooded male from having sex in a situation like that," said Brother Vitiver.

"You wouldn't even know about this if I hadn't told you." I didn't want to sound unrepentant, but I struggled to understand the actual cause of my disfellowshipping. Was I being punished for my sins? For not going all the way with my sins? For confessing?

"Jehovah makes things known sooner or later," Brother Slice said.

"Okay. I hope I can make it back," I said, defeated and broken.

"We also feel like too much time has passed since the incident to reflect repentance," Brother Froyer elaborated.

"I get it," I said as I held up my hand. *Maybe that had something to do with how embarrassing talking about this was.*

"Your presence for the announcement would show that you respect the decision and reflect the right condition of heart," said Brother Slice. "If you feel that we have acted in error, you may submit an appeal letter within the next seven days."

"Alright."

I was present for my disfellowshipping and Kim's public reproof. The congregation accepted the news of my disfellowshipping dispassionately, the same way they reacted to my fellowship in the years leading up to this. There was no real discernible difference when I was being shunned – at least now there was a *reason* I was being ignored. I almost preferred it. My best friends shunned me, but they had no problem asking my mother to ask me if they could borrow $1,500. My mother still spoke to me since I lived with her, but, per the rules of disfellowshipping, we did not discuss spiritual things.

My first reinstatement letter emphasized my emotional state, that I had been unhappy, depressed, and alienated since the death of my father. I spoke of how that state of affairs made it all the more imperative to me that I refocus my faith and dedication to Jehovah. I went as far as to express that I felt it should be acknowledged that I was attempting to return to a way of life that had always been unkind and unwelcoming to me. In this letter, perhaps more than any other specific time, I tried to establish a sympathetic bond with the elders of my congregation. Both the letter and my request to be reinstated were rejected summarily.

After the rejection, I numbly searched out and found an apostate reinstatement letter template online. The second letter was brief, disingenuous, and obsequious. It was accepted without reservation and I was reinstated after 18 months of shunning. I earnestly tried to find a renewed zeal for preaching and works following my reinstatement, but it was always hollow. I would never feel accepted in that congregation. Shortly after my reinstatement, I switched to Cragwell's sister congregation. The first time I went out in service and knocked on doors there, the elder I was paired with asked if I was "the kid with really bad mental problems."

Eight years later, Kim called my mother and told her that I owed her money. I had no idea what she was talking about and disregarded the incident. Two days after that, I received a letter without a return address that insulted me and told me that I was going to give Kim what she was owed "or else." The following morning, there were tire tracks through the grass behind our house running up to my car. Three of my tires were slashed, paint bubbled and ran from under where Kim had poured paint stripper, but the most disturbing part was the dead rabbit we found in my backyard with a single, clean puncture wound about the size of a pencil.

When Kim's father heard about what had happened, he asked to see the letter. After confirming to me that it was Kim's handwriting, he paid me damages for my car. I felt sorry for him in the exchange. He was clearly mortified at his daughter's behavior, and I had always respected the man to a degree. A few weeks later, my mother called me.

"Listen, I wanted to let you know that Kim is dead."

"Oh?" I wasn't sure if my tone of voice was appropriate. *That's a relief.*

"Yeah, she'd been abusing pills and alcohol for some time. She lost her job, her license, and eventually even showed up to traffic court drunk. That's when they prescribed some court-mandated medication that would make her sick if she drank again."

"How did she die?"

"She aspirated and drowned in a pool of her own vomit."

"Imagine how much you'd have to vomit to fill a pool."

"This isn't funny!" my mother scolded. "She died disfellowshipped. *Hopefully* she gets a resurrection."

I didn't think it was funny that Kim was dead either, but I didn't know how else to react to the news. I certainly wasn't surprised. I had long suspected Kim of being capable of anything, after our experience in Ohio. Reflecting on it, I felt worse for Kim's father than I did for her. Kim had long suffered from a severe substance abuse problem. Dying disfellowshipped meant that she had been estranged and shunned from her father and friends in the time leading up to her death, the absolute last thing that she or her family needed. But Kim was ostracized from her exclusive social group at her time of greatest need, for the very reasons *of* her need.

Not too long after my mother called to inform me of Kim's death, two other Jehovah's Witnesses I knew died. The first, William, had become notably depressed and withdrawn after the death of his mother. He turned to alcohol to numb the pain. Eventually he drove onto a military camp and shot himself in the head. I can still remember his little girl asking if her "daddy would be in paradise". The other, Carl, shot himself in his work truck on his lunch break. What was the congregation's response to these three substance-abuse deaths and suicides in such a short period? To hold meetings to frankly discuss the problems of depression, hopelessness, and substance dependency? No – my congregants barely acknowledged these deaths and when the topic was brought up it was quickly changed.

I felt myself slipping into the same hole that claimed Kim, William, and Carl. Constantly drinking, never drunk, simply warding off the fear of Armageddon and the despair of facing reality while sober. I felt like my life had no prospects. No girlfriend, living with my widowed mother to help with chores. Lacking earthly ambition, shunned by my spiritual and social group that enforced their exclusivity despite excluding me. Working a thankless job I hated to address a growing mountain of debt. In desperation, I turned again to the elders with my concerns. I was told to wait on a call that would come in the next week.

"Hi," I answered.

"What's going on?" Brother Dunbar asked.

"I'm really not doing well." When I had asked to speak to one of the elders, I was disappointed to find out it would be brother Dunbar. Brother Dunbar was not someone that I respected or whose advice I wanted. He routinely mispronounced words or invented new ones and he paid illegal immigrants under the table in his construction business.

"Why?" Brother Dunbar sounded like he was chewing food.

"I'm not happy. Studying, meetings, praying...none of them help."

He gave a grunt of exasperation. "I hated studying for years! You have to pray to Jehovah, He'll make you enjoy those things."

"It hasn't worked so far. Nobody notices when I miss meetings and when I'm there I'm never spoken to."

"Jehovah's spirit is there, with your brothers and sisters! We are not supposed to forsake gathering together."

"It's like I don't exist. I want to die."

"What?" He had finally dropped his elder voice and sounded like I was talking to a person.

"I think about buying a gun and a hollow point bullet so it will blow the back of my head off. I'll get drunk first, to thin my blood, and I'll find some water to stand in so if the gunshot doesn't kill me I'll drown. If you fail to plan, you plan to fail." I didn't mean to reveal this to the elder when I had started the phone call, but once I started to talk about it, it tumbled out of me mechanically.

Brother Dunbar paused for some time. "What is it that you want?" He sounded more flummoxed than concerned.

"Encouragement." Some compassion. "It would be nice if someone invited me out in service or even noticed if I was at meetings."

"You...you really don't have it bad, do you? You live with your mom, you don't have a wife or kids. You don't have any responsibility or anyone depending on you. You really have an easy life." His irritation was evident in his voice now.

"What?" I was genuinely taken aback. *Is this what I get for trying?*

"You want a brother to come and get you dressed? Do you want somebody to drive you to meetings and to meet for service?" His tone was gratuitously mocking, dripping with cruelty.

I managed a quick, colorless "I need to go", as I fumbled the phone back onto the receiver. I stood there, head bowed, hand on the phone, for some time.

I didn't want to live with my mother, I felt obligation to help her out with chores and money since she was a widow. I had a lot of debt. I wanted to be married. I had responsibilities. My mother depended on me. I told my mother about how obtuse Brother Dunbar was.

"Wait on Jehovah," she said.

That was the night that I decided I was going to drink as much alcohol as I could from that point forward. It was an absurd decision, but I made it rationally in response to the facts of my environment. Chugging a beer before meetings, vodka before going out in service, I made a point to be drunk as often as possible. The only way I could make sense of my feelings was that Jehovah had rejected me through His elders. He didn't want me. The coping mechanisms that were prescribed to the spiritual man – prayer, studying, reading the Bible – would never work for me because of my inherent and irredeemable unworthiness. I deserved to die.

Physically In, Mentally Questioning

An implement of circumstance, I know no divide. In every thought I possess you somehow reside.
Wallowing affinity, swallowing infinity.
Broken by and always for, ambivalent I decompose. Beloved Judas, my beloved. What I trusted I suppose.
Forgiveness is giving nothing. Everything has lost its grace.
Better left unsaid and hateful. Crestfallen look upon her face.
Caesar trusted, demons lusted.
Crumbling beneath the brunt. Forgotten bluster, truest friend stabs the front.
Acrid speech, vitriol spray. Three-cord thread begins to fray.
Jesus Christ will you deliver?
Every sheltered broken message, buried deep and giving way.
How did we become this? Granite ash flicked away.
No division, bifurcated whole. I am human, we are standing. You're my favorite soul.

I remember the first time I saw Nova, I remember the door she was standing in front of. It was Koi No Yokan. Hopelessly, irrevocably her visage was burnt into my retinas. Nova gave me a ride home the day Kim destroyed my car and I met her little boy Ian. Nova was gorgeous and we had instant chemistry but she wasn't a Jehovah's Witness. I witnessed to Nova and to my surprise she showed interest, it felt like evidence of Jehovah's blessing that He would use me to draw someone to Him.

After our first meeting together, the congregation surrounded Nova, introducing themselves and assuring her that she was welcome. While it was nice to see the congregation so accepting of someone I'd brought, I couldn't suppress a wayward envious feeling. They had never been so accepting of me.

When Nova asked about studying, I recommended her to study with Sister Rizaldo. Her husband was the young, cool elder at Paleland. Nova began studying, bringing Ian to meetings, and they both began going out in service. She made quick progress and was soon talking of baptism. Nova and Ian began spending more and more time with my mother and me. It was the happiest time of my life. I dreamed of living forever with Nova and introducing her and Ian to my father after he was resurrected. All was bright until one Sunday afternoon, when members of the popular clique at Paleland invited Nova and Ian over.

"People asked if we were dating," Nova said afterward.

"What people?" I asked.

"Ian and I went swimming at the Rizaldos'. There were a lot of people there." I felt my heart constrict at the mention of the Rizaldo's pool. Studying with Sister Rizaldo was one thing, but I knew how loose talk could get at their social functions.

"What did you tell them?"

"I said we were friends at the moment, but we'd be open to it later, after I get baptized."

"Okay." *Nothing wrong with that.* My heart soared at her response.

"You know, people acted surprised when I told them you were the one that witnessed to me."

"Oh." I wasn't surprised.

She paused for a moment. "It seems like people who've been disfellowshipped are treated as lesser." Nova observed this quietly, her gaze directed across the yard, at nothing in particular.

"That's just their imperfection." *Please don't leave.* "Did you talk to Sister Rizaldo about it?"

"I did, and she told me to reconsider spending so much time with spiritually weak ones. She meant you." Her voice carried the edge of an unplaceable emotion.

"Yeah." I wasn't strong in the truth, but it didn't mean I loved Nova any less.

It was confounding to me that Paleland congregation was so indifferent to me while I suffered, yet so intrusive when I was happy. I was hurt that Sister Rizaldo had intimated to Nova that I wasn't good enough for her. I was livid because there was no scriptural basis for me and Nova to be in trouble so I decided that I would fight for Nova and for Ian. I wasn't going to allow my judgmental congregation to make them lose out on eternal life. I trusted in Jehovah!

I felt that I was in the right and if I would just weather this one last, big storm I would be rewarded with a loving wife in Nova. I had struggled for so long but I wanted to make Jehovah happy.

The following Thursday, Nova and I were summoned to meet with Brothers Rizaldo and Slice. The subject of their inquiry was obvious to Nova and myself before we entered the room.

"We aren't dating, people have spread the lie that we are. That's slander," I said.

"Her car *is* in your driveway a lot," said Brother Rizaldo noncommittally.

"Is this the mob? Am I under surveillance?" I asked contemptuously. "I'm *thirty-three* and she's *twenty-seven*!"

"We are never too old for Jehovah's standards." The brother's tone was stern.

"You can't be counseled for something you haven't even done, right?" I could feel myself getting heated.

"We're not here to accuse you two of wrongdoing," Brother Slice said.

"Then what is the point of this?" I demanded.

"If your actions are bothering the consciences of others in the congregation, then it cannot be allowed."

"What about not rushing to take offense?" Nova's voice was conciliatory, but her expression showed she understood that the verdict had passed.

"You two can still see each other," Brother Slice reassured us. "After meetings, at the hall. It can't be what it was." I looked at Brother Slice's false smile, then over to Nova's tear-streaked face. I still don't know which was worse.

"We have to remain loyal!" My mother always staunchly defended the elders.

"We *are*. What they're saying isn't Biblical," I said.

"It's about loyalty to Jehovah and to those He's appointed."

"*You* told me about how all the elders but one got removed at Cragwell back in the 70s." She blinked, then resumed her earlier tone.

"We *have* to obey the elders!"

"We didn't do anything wrong! This is bullshit!" It shouldn't have surprised me that my mother would take the elder's side yet again. But in this case, where we had done nothing wrong – I couldn't contain my resentment over her choosing the congregation over me any longer.

"We are told that the instruction we receive might not make sense from a human point of view."

"That's about Armageddon! It's not the same thing!"

"We have to stay loyal!" My mother was getting shrill and flat-out yelling at me now.

"We did *nothing* wrong! This is bullshit! It's discouraging me and Nova. And what about Ian?" She grasped her hair in her hands.

"*Micah*!" My mother's eyes bulged as she screamed. "I have to remain loyal!" She seemed to be at her wit's end.

"Loyal to *what*?" I screamed. "Loyal to some bullshit rule Brother Slice pulled out of his ass? What about loyalty to your son?"

"I want you *OUT* of my house by the end of the weekend!" She turned and stormed away from me, still screaming and wringing her hair.

"I give you all my fucking money! I don't have anywhere to go!"

"Call someone you work with!"

"Who? At least give me until I get paid next Friday! Mom, please, the only person I can ask for help is the one person I'm not allowed to talk to!"

"Figure it out!" my mother said as she rushed out the door.

"What the fuck is *wrong* with you?" I screamed, but my mother couldn't hear me as she backed out of the driveway.

I went to Nova's and talked to her about what had happened, and she told me I could move in with her. Nova and Ian were the family I'd always wanted. When I lost my virginity to Nova that night, I knew I'd be disfellowshipped a second time, that Jehovah would cut me off from his Holy Spirit, and I'd be shunned by my mother and my few friends. I suspected I might not be forgiven. I was willing to never speak to my father, mother and the few friends I had ever again. I rejected Jehovah and gave up immortality on a paradise Earth for Nova.

My mother acted surprised when Nova and I pulled up to pack up my things, looking at me through tears.

"Where did you expect me to go?" I asked. Only my mother knew that I'd moved in with Nova.

Two days later, Brother Rizaldo texted me to ask me to meet with the elders.

"With matters such as this, we have to consider what you have done to right the wrong," Brother Slice's voice droned from his seat between Brother Rizaldo and Brother Prist.

"What have I done to right the wrong of having sex with Nova?" I asked.

"What have you done to correct the matter and show that you're repentant?"

"We're going to get married as soon as we can." Their reception of this fact was muted.

"Have you made any efforts to leave this woman's home?" Rizaldo intervened, his demeanor more inquisitive than admonitory.

"No." Regardless of his tone, I was offended by the question. "I love her."

"Do you love Jehovah?" Prist's voice carried a favored edge that he always assumed at disciplinary meetings.

"Yes," I said, more robotically than I would have liked.

"What are you willing to do to protect your relationship with Him?"

I was getting frustrated. "I don't have anywhere to go."

"You don't have *anywhere* to go? There are shelters for people like you. You could call the police and tell them that you are destitute."

It was too early in the conversation to be incredulous, but I didn't care. "Instead of living with the woman I love, I should move into a *homeless shelter*?"

"Yes! To maintain your relationship with Jehovah!" Brother Prist hissed the word "relationship".

"No." I shook my head.

During the brief pause, two brothers exchanged glances with pursed lips. They seemed unsurprised with the tenor of the meeting. "Regarding the immorality, was it an isolated incident?"

"No." My tone was hard.

I knew I would be disfellowshipped before the elders dismissed me. I was told for the second time in my life that I was going to be disfellowshipped, that my attendance at the announcement would indicate the correct attitude, and that I could submit an appeal letter within a week. But I didn't go to meeting that night because I didn't respect them. I stayed at home with my new family. When Nova and I eloped, Ian was my best man. Nova told her closest friends and her co-workers that we were married, but apart from Ian, she didn't tell her family. Our marriage remained a secret for over a year. I imagine it would have been difficult to tell your family and friends that you have married a man so he could be reinstated as soon as possible into your new religion, a religion that wanted you to distance yourself from every non-member. No pain before or since that secret has ever hurt me as viscerally, and I was incapable of perceiving it as anything other than absolute rejection.

I didn't hate my new extended family but I did believe they were doomed. I never forbid my family from spending time with them, but they knew I didn't approve and that it worried me. It isn't possible to view people as anything other than disposable when you routinely pray for their destruction, when you look forward to the day that God will destroy them. I hated telling Nova and Ian to choose Jehovah over their family because I knew how awful it felt when my mother chose Jehovah over me.

When I found the homemade Christmas ornaments Nova's dead grandmother had made, I pressured her into throwing them away.

"But these were the last thing she gave me before she died," Nova said tearfully.

"You don't need the ornaments. You can get her back if you're loyal," I reasoned.

"You do it. I can't," Nova said as she walked away.

I have no way of knowing, but I don't think it was any easier for me to put those ornaments in the can than it would have been for her.

My sexuality was repressed from the time it developed to the moment I lost my virginity. I remember sleepless nights with raging hormones, praying to my God for my erection to go away. I remember the guilt of living a double life whenever I would look at pornography or masturbate. I would write down confessions, lists of "sins," and tell the elders. I felt guilt for desiring my wife, as if I was objectifying the woman I was supposed to respect most. My desires felt sinful, perverted and shameful. I was confused. I trace that confusion back to years of sitting next to my parents in meetings hearing about beastiality, masturbation, prostitution, infidelity, incest, and rape. One talk in particular stands out.

"Brothers and sisters, when I use the phrase digital sex, I'm not talking about technology. I'm referring to these." Brother Mitchell held up his hand and waggled his sausage fingers. "Acts like oral and anal sex are all homosexual in nature, akin to beastiality. These things go against the way Jehovah designed us. Jehovah wants us to enjoy sex, he designed our bodies to work that way. Would we really want to go and defile our marriage beds? Absolutely not!"

Everyone in the audience knew who Brother Mitchell was speaking about, the brother and sister had been publicly reproved a few weeks before. I noticed the sister's head was hung in her seat a few rows ahead of me. As Brother Mitchell spoke I stared at my thighs and imagined falling through the design on my dress pants.

The elder's words rattled around in my head when I slept with Nova, and I could feel Jehovah watching us. I worried that if Nova and I tried oral sex, it would somehow mean that I was gay and deserved to die. I worried that if *I* deserved to die, Jehovah would kill my family too. I worried that even having the *desire* to try oral sex was a symptom of latent homosexuality. Just as I believed apostate material could warp my mind, I believed "homosexual" acts could lead to homosexuality.

"He's struggling to breathe," Doctor Pratz said, referring to Cyrus, my newborn son. Nova was bleeding heavily from the episiotomy, Cyrus was fighting to breathe after just seven minutes of life, and Ian was in the waiting room with my mother – who was still shunning me.

"We need to fly him to the children's hospital." a nurse told us as she wheeled Cyrus into the room in what looked like a little Lucite coffin. I reached through the opening and touched his tiny arm.

"I love you, son," I said for the first time. *If he's gay, God will kill him*. I groaned as I pushed the ugly thought away.

"You're still disfellowshipped, but I'll drive you to the other hospital." my mother said. I could tell she was worried, but she spoke mechanically to me.

"Okay." I replied dolefully.

As we drove, my mother brought up blood transfusions and I thought of my father. I knew I wanted Cyrus as soon as Nova told me she was pregnant. I knew I would be ready to kill for him the moment I laid eyes on him.

"You need to call the elders in case the doctors want to give him blood," my mother repeated. "They can send a liaison committee."

"I'm disfellowshipped. They won't even talk to me!" Even in the state I was in, I could feel the wrath bubbling up. The fear of another preventable loss that I was supposed to accept as Jehovah's will.

"You need to call them. I can help."

I appreciated my mother's help driving, but her obstinance at that moment sickened and infuriated me. "I need to talk to Nova," I said. Nova and I briefly exchanged only the most necessary details about Cyrus' health before I suggested that we call to elders to come to the hospital in case Cyrus needed a blood transfusion. Nova hung up on me and I'm thankful that she did. I told my mother that I wouldn't call the elders to the hospital unless Nova was okay with it. I imagined Jehovah killing Cyrus and Nova in front of me before He killed me. It's plausible that I would have let Cyrus die if he'd needed a blood transfusion that night. The elders would have supported me, even though I was disfellowshipped and shunned, as I martyred my son through neglect.

I had worried something like this might happen so I wrote a poem about the son I feared Jehovah wouldn't save.

12.15.2017.

Son you begin.

7 minutes in.

A lifetime of fear.

Don't leave me here.

At one time, I believed there was worldwide organization, consistency, and unity among Jehovah's Witnesses. But when trying to get reinstated, I myself experienced inconsistencies between the Paleland and Benjamin congregations – which share a building.

"It's too soon," Brother Lynn said after I turned in my first letter. "When you roll your sleeves up and expose your tattoos are you trying to be rebellious, look scary, or offend others?"

"It's over 90 degrees. I've had most of my tattoos for more than a decade. I've rolled my sleeves up at meetings, assemblies and conventions. Would you like me to wear long sleeves?"

"I didn't say that. Regardless, more time needs to pass." I could feel my anger surge at this elder who barred my fellowship and lacked the temerity to even say why.

I went to a pop culture convention with my family shortly before I turned in my second reinstatement letter. I dressed up as Bane and Ian and I both had fake weapons. When Nova posted a picture of our costumes on Facebook, Sister Slice left a comment about how shameful it was for Jehovah's Witnesses to 'like' the post. Nova deleted Sister Slice's comment, so then she left a second one. When I submitted my second reinstatement letter, I was surprised that the post came up.

"What do you think someone thinks of you when they see you dressed like that, carrying a toy shotgun?" Brother Lynn asked.

"That I'm a geek," I said. I knew I wasn't getting off to a good start, but my hope in a fair process had long since faded.

"You don't think that it makes you look like a lover of violence?"

"No," I said as I shifted in my seat, making a face. "There are elders in this hall that own handguns."

"Why didn't you dress up like Batman?"

"Because the villains are cooler. You do realize Batman brutalizes criminals? Have you seen the movies?" I already sounded exasperated, but I found the line of questioning to be ridiculous. I faced an assignment of guilt at the hands of a religious tribunal for the sin of going to a cosplay convention with my family.

Brother Lynn pursed his lips. "Yes."

"Then what are we talking about? Aren't you a lover of violence as well?"

"I don't dress up like characters."

"So you conceal your true nature? By that rationale, I can watch gay pornography, but I can't have gay sex."

"No." Brother Lynn seemed resigned to his decision, but carried on. "What kind of example are you setting for your sons?"

"I'm being a fun dad," I said, incredulous. "You're not going to reinstate me, are you?"

"Not today."

"When I went to Paleland, I dressed as Joker all the time and it was never an issue. I even showed up to an elder's house dressed up like a homicidal clown! I'm guessing Sister Slice told her husband and he told you. She was harassing my wife online with her idle hands.

Why is this an issue here but not in Paleland congregation? It sure seems like it's just your way of keeping me out with a conscience matter."

"That is not the case." Brother Lynn was keeping composed, but I could tell I was long out of his good graces. I didn't care.

"Conscience matters abound. I've been counseled for wearing too many dark colors. Well, Brother, I have to tell you that your khaki suit, pastel shirt, and floral tie look very homosexual and trigger my conscience. What about all the morbid obesity in this congregation? Aren't elders supposed to be men of modest habits?"

"Yes."

"Only one of you isn't overweight, and there is an elder in this hall whose stomach hangs below his knees." I was digging a hole, but I didn't care. I was almost enjoying it. "You can call me a nasty person but you can't claim his eating habits are *modest*. He is not a man of modest habits, therefore he should be removed. I'm leaving before you have to eat your dinner through a straw."

I was quietly dismissed without further incident. Unsurprisingly, I was not reinstated following my second meeting.

When I wrote my third reinstatement letter, I didn't figure I would be reinstated that time either. I was beginning to wonder if it would ever happen.

"Do you know what it means to be brazen?" Brother Lynn asked.

"Akin to shameless, I believe," I answered.

"It's a quality that Christians should avoid." His voice was stern and cold, like a father who relishes the position of lecturing a wayward child.

"Yeah."

"You were rather brazen with your disrespect when we last spoke."

"I was," I said. *I was honest and I don't regret what I said.*

"The Bible says that elders are worthy of double honor."

"Yeah." *Elders can be removed from their positions.*

"You need to consider how you speak to the elders and how you speak about them. You called an elder disgusting when we last met."

"I said he was morbidly obese, which he is. I didn't call him disgusting."

"Do you think he doesn't know? Do you think he isn't aware that he's disgusting?" Brother Lynn collected himself with a little gesture to reseat his glasses.

"No," I said, confused. *Why does he keep using this word I never used?*

"You need to be careful with the words you use, especially when they're directed at the elders." Brother Lynn peered at me through thick frames.

"You're correct. I spoke out of turn. I am sorry, I apologize." *Asshole.*

After taking me in for a moment, Brother Lynn broke his silence. "Wait a little while longer."

"Okay," I said, smiling. *All Jehovah's Witnesses are equal, but some are more equal than others.*

After I submitted my fourth reinstatement letter, the elders at Benjamin congregation allowed me to meet with Paleland's elders.

"I'm surprised you haven't submitted a letter before now!" Brother Slice exclaimed.

"This is my fourth letter. I've been denied three times."

"Your fourth? Denied by who?"

"The elders at Benjamin."

"That's not how Jehovah's organization works," Brother Slice chided.

"That's how it's been working."

"The elders that disfellowship you decide whether or not it's time for a reinstatement!"

"Unless other elders supersede them and preclude them from making that decision. You know, the second time I turned in a letter I was denied because your wife had been harassing my wife on social media. She owes Nova an apology."

"That is between them. This conversation is about your reinstatement."

"I'm not even sure I want to get reinstated." I was surprised to hear myself say it out loud to Brother Slice, but the feelings had been long dormant.

"If you don't want to be a part of Jehovah's organization, that's your decision. If you want to hate me for the rest of your life, you can! You just need to let me know what you want to do."

"I never said I hate you."

When I met with Paleland's elders, Brother Slice asked me how I felt about offending the consciences of my brothers and sisters. I told the elders that I regretted prioritizing my wants over Jehovah and the congregation. Brother Slice told me that he had never heard me express regret or show concern for others before, and then he told me I would be reinstated. After 25 months of shunning, I was reinstated as a married man and a father.

Physically In, Mentally Out

The great fear inspiring day of Jehovah. I've gotta tell ya, I think it might be overkill.
Would you take a look at these panicky, monkey moron, inchworms?
Clawing, crambling, scrambling and there isn't any bread at the supermarket. Stores have gone biblical over snow.
A constant transfusion of white knuckle, teeth grinding, paralytic terror.
Low T? Vaginal dryness? Bankruptcy? Too much hair or too little? Erectile enhancement systems, male enhancement, depression, bi-polar, AD-HD, herpes, school shootings, shingles, high blood pressure, insurance quotes, mesothelioma. Meth labs in cars, in traffic, at lights!
A side effect of my inhaler is death by asthma. Government approved!
You need the new phone.
T.V. on! Stabbed, shot, beaten, robbed, arson, breaking and entering, rape. The fear lullaby.
Filed away so I can record the apocalypse with my camera.
Sucking suck, biting on the capitalist teat. Chomping, buying in.
Go back to sleep, your mouth is filled around that stupid grin.

The combined absurdity of the 45th president's election campaign and the onset of the COVID-19 pandemic reinforced my belief that Armageddon was imminent. A lifetime of fear had primed me for a reptilian-brain response as I watched prophecy being fulfilled around me. I loved Nova, Ian and Cyrus more than Jehovah, and I figured since I was the spiritual head of my family, my destruction meant their destruction. I also knew Nova didn't want to serve Jehovah and I didn't want to live without her. How could it be paradise without *her*? Nova's disillusionment with serving Jehovah had been cemented when Sister Rizaldo spoke to her about re-piercing her nose. Brother Rizaldo and I had been friends at one time – he was the first person I told about Nova, and he was who I turned to when I worried that Nova was coming to meetings for me instead of for Jehovah. I recommended his wife to study with Nova – before he served on the judicial committee that disfellowshipped me for the second time. I called him up.

"Hello?" Brother Rizaldo answered.

"What's this about your wife telling my wife she is worldly because she re-pierced her nose?"

"She was trying to adjust her thinking."

"It made her feel like absolute garbage. You people keep pushing and pushing and then you wonder why people leave."

"What does her piercing her nose say about her spirituality?"

"She hadn't been out in service in months! I'm the spiritual head, if there is some issue it should be brought to me."

"She's studying with Nova."

"I'm her husband. You've destroyed her faith. Do you know years ago your wife told Nova not to spend time with me because I wasn't spiritual enough? I need Brother Dunbar's number."

"I didn't know that. What do you need his number for?"

"Because he mocked me when I was suicidal. What if he's treated others that way?"

"You have evidence he's treated others similarly?"

"He did it to me. Why am I not enough? He needs to be confronted."

"This is probably something better left to Jehovah."

"I thought if we had a problem with our brother, we were supposed to talk to him about it. If you won't give me his number I'll just get it from someone else."

"How're you doing?" Brother Dunbar answered.

"Not so great," I said. "Do you recall when we spoke and I told you I wanted to die?"

"Yup!" The fucker sounded *chipper*.

"You were dismissive, you belittled my problems and you mocked me by asking if I needed help getting dressed."

"Nah. That didn't happen." I was awestruck at his tone. He sounded so happy, so full of himself, so self-confident in his ability to gaslight me. He didn't need to act surprised at what I was saying – I was *supposed* to believe his account of events, so I *would*.

"What?"

"Ask Brother Slice, he was there."

"Now wait a minute, we spoke on the phone. Are you telling me he was in the background listening, without me knowing?"

"We spoke in person."

"No...we...you liar! Don't ever speak to me again." I felt like I was falling into myself, through myself. This was a cover up. I heard my phone ringing and I answered it without looking at it.

"You don't hang up on me, boy!" Brother Dunbar said sternly.

"Oh, what the fuck?!" I screamed as I slammed a knife into the counter. "You will *never* tell me what to do again, you ineffectual simpleton. Do you know how much I dread sitting in meetings hearing you mispronounce words? Elders are commanded to help suffering people! You'll be judged twice as harshly so enjoy that *glorious* day! People that mock suicidal people deserve to die. I know you have cancer and I hope it eats you slow. I know your wife had a miscarriage and I'm glad that baby missed out on being raised by a piece of shit like you. Come to my apartment and call me boy, I'll beat you until your legs fall the *fuck* off!"

I felt empowered after I hung up the phone. I stood over the sink as my chest heaved. I had to tell my mom what was going on. I heard a knock at the door and hoped it was Nova. I just wanted to hug her and tell her I loved her and we would figure everything out. But when I opened the door, I saw six policemen. *What the fuck?* The officers forced their way inside when they saw the blood – there was blood *everywhere*. I had sliced my pinkie finger when I stabbed the counter and hadn't even realized I was bleeding.

"Did you try and hurt yourself?" an officer asked.

"No. I was not going to lower myself into a warm bath and slit my pinkies." The officers, unamused, were surrounding me and forcing me out the door.

"You need to go to the hospital.," said another officer.

"I'll go to the one down the road."

"No. You need to come with us." The officers were driving me down the stairs.

"My wife is an R.N., this is unnecessary." I saw a gurney waiting for me, multiple officers put their hands on my shoulders and gently pushed me down. "Look, I am not going with you." I stood back up, flailing my arms as I did.

"Don't throw your blood at us! We don't want AIDs."

"You look like you've sucked some dick," I said. "You probably already have it." All of the officers simultaneously grabbed me and slammed me onto the gurney.

I arrived at a stress center and told every staff member that I wasn't suicidal, I'd just suggested a cop was a homosexual. When I met with the counselor, I told him I was a Jehovah's Witness and I was struggling with my faith. He told me he had experience with a lot of ex Jehovah's Witnesses. I was released from the stress center after 72 hours.

The following week, as I was climbing into the shower, my phone rang. An unfamiliar number was calling.

"Hello," Brother Robbins said. "I want you to know that brother Williams is on the line as well."

"How are you today?" Brother Williams inquired.

"I'm fine, I was about to get into the shower," I said.

"We can give you a minute to get dressed," Brother Robbins offered.

"I don't have long. I'll just stand here with my balls out," I replied.

"We appreciate you taking the time to answer our call. We are all living busy lives, we'll try not to take up too much of your time. We are calling about the events of last Wednesday."

"When I called brother Dunbar? Is he in the background listening?"

"Yes, and no."

"I remember calling him. I also remember him mocking me for being suicidal and how none of the other elders seemed like that was even worth acknowledging. Did you call to disfellowship me over the phone?" *I'm going to die at Armageddon.*

"We're just gathering information at the moment. We'd like to hear your side of things."

"I don't know why. You're going to take his side. I cursed at him, insulted him, I said I didn't care that he has cancer and I don't. I said his dead baby was better off dead than being raised by him. He mocks depressed, suicidal people."

"Did you make any threatening remarks?"

"I invited him over with the intention of kicking his ass."

"What course of action do you feel you should take?" Brother Williams asked.

"What do you mean?" I asked. "Are you suggesting that I apologize to him? Mocking a depressed, suicidal person is abuse. Do you want me to apologize to my abuser?"

"We're talking about being peaceable." Brother Robbins interjected.

"That is not happening."

"If that's the way you feel about the matter, we don't feel that it would be appropriate for you to physically attend meetings once the pandemic is over," Brother Williams said.

"I'm banned from the Hall?" I asked incredulously. I didn't know that was a thing.

"You are welcome to attend online meetings."

Brother Slice corroborating brother Dunbar's lies had massive ramifications. The stories I'd read about elders protecting pedophiles rang true.

"I'm banned from physically attending meetings," I said into the phone.

"Are you surprised?" my mother asked.

"Yeah." *Why aren't you?*

"The brothers have never had to deal with anything like this before. They had to call Bethel to ask them how to handle things."

"Mom...what are you talking about?"

"You threatened to kill the congregation!"

"I did not do that. I'm not stupid. If I wanted to kill the congregation, I sure wouldn't give them a hint I was planning to."

"Oh, that's great."

"I'm just making a point."

"I don't have to listen to this."

"You're right, you don't. But please, I'm your son! I've seen a video of one of the Governing Body buying a cart filled with expensive alcohol bottles. How does a Bethelite who has taken a vow of poverty have money for that? It has to be donation money! Children are told to give their ice cream money to Jehovah!"

"Look at what they do with the CGI in those superhero movies, apostates could have faked that."

"Oh mom, no."

"I am not listening to this!"

"They're lying! Mom, you've got to listen to me. Mom? Mom!"

My mother didn't listen to me because she couldn't; she had hung up the phone. When I called her back, my number was blocked. I grabbed my father's knife and pressed it hard into my forearm. The searing pain centered me, and I realized I was screaming, trying to keep the thoughts from forming in my brain. Nova was beside me trying to stop the bleeding, Ian looked concerned and Cyrus screamed along with me. The cut in my arm smiled at me and then, as if it had suddenly remembered its purpose, started pumping blood out of me.

We lost our childcare due to Covid and we had nobody that could or would help us with our boys. Nova called my mother and asked her to help us.

"I'm in my 60s and I'm susceptible," my mother said.

"You are a *cunt*," I said after I snatched the phone out of Nova's hand. "All those bullshit stories you told about sticking together during the last days. You're refusing to help us when we need you most. Dad would have cared. I buried the wrong parent."

Eventually I quit my job, though I should have quit earlier. My health had been deteriorating as my drinking escalated. I was going to pain management, I fell frequently, I sometimes needed a cane to walk and my urine was routinely dark orange or red. Often I didn't even wake up hungover – I was still drunk. I was going to apply for disability, be a stay at home dad and make up for so many memories I had missed with my father.

Nova was starting a new job at a hospital and I was filled with pride. I took Cyrus to the grocery store in my muscle car and we listened to German metal. That night I made ribs and baked potatoes for my family. I was drunk like I usually was. I had been drunk nearly every day for seven years. After dinner I started arguing with Ian over dishes, and everything went black.

Physically Out, Mentally In

A siren cutting the air. Born anew in unseen atmosphere.
Hellfire curls around the billowing form of a seraph. Weight and I am just about sick.
Asinine rationalizations, stiff with conceit, claiming doubt, strength and independence.
The diametric opposite of your bullshit persona, I don't want you for an echo.
No segue, these lies and flighty theories are mutually exclusive.
No love like first love. I've forgotten that passion. Everyone does.
If every pain, sorrow, mistake and punishment was so I might save you it was worthwhile.
You just sit there like a cold, sociopath bastard. Don't say what I want to hear. Sycophant.
The mystery you think you are, I was. This is a betrayal, an indulgence of self. You lie.
My love is unconditional, my friendship isn't. Wait, I'm sick.
This wears on me as you sit there arrogant. Pride goes before a fall.
So throw it all away, I will not bare witness. You don't get to apologize for ruining my day.
Not to me, to your family or yourself. Be a man.
Own what you do my dear brother, my child.
I am sick, I am just about sick of you. Smudging black and white.
No juxtapositions, only complication. Generalities and you lied.
You are Cain and I am able.

Jail was a fermenting stew of offenses to every sense. The hinges of the rubber-room door creaked heinously as it opened. My stomach and head churned out of sync.

"Time to get up!" Officer Wurst said as he flashed me a rictus grin. Stiff and hungover, I struggled to stand. Wurst extended his sausage fingers and I hesitantly grabbed his hand. The anti-suicide smock's worn Velcro pulled at all three places it attached as Wurst hoisted me upright. Outside of the rubber room, a bookish officer took my mugshot.

"Do you know why you're here?" Officer Stalwart asked as he took my picture.

"No." I said dryly.

"You've been charged with battery and strangulation."

"Who did I do that to?" As I spoke, reality loosened its grip, and when Stalwart said Ian's name, reality let go completely. All I heard were garbled vowels as Stalwart wiped ink from my fingers. I asked if Ian was okay, but Stalwart only responded by escorting me back to the padded cell. *Please don't leave me alone,* I thought as the door slammed shut. I slumped against the wall and down onto the floor. I was cold, but my neck hurt so I took off the turtle suit and rolled it into a makeshift pillow. *How badly did I hurt Ian?* The question repeated itself until I fell asleep.

The cell door opened gently the second time. Wurst stepped into the room, then back out.

"Get dressed and come to the door," Officer Wurst said.

"Yes sir." I unrolled the turtle suit, put it on, and stepped into the doorway.

"Hi, I'm Daxton and I'm the social worker here at the jail," said a familiar face.

"Hi," I said as I looked at the ground. I wasn't sure if I wanted my former co-worker to recognize me or not.

"You weren't doing the best when you came in last night, how're you feeling?" Daxton said kindly.

"Okay."

"You told the officers last night you wanted to die."

"I don't remember anything from last night." *You don't remember me.*

"Are you still feeling suicidal?"

"No," I lied.

"I'm going to sign off to get you some regular clothes and out of this cell."

"Thank you," I said quietly.

"What size do you wear?" Wurst asked.

"I don't know, I usually wear a medium. I've never been in jail before."

Wurst rolled his eyes as he shut the door. Daxton reminded me that my past was real, and I feared Wurst was predicting my future. The cell door barely creaked at all the next time it was opened, because someone had *flung* it open with considerable force. An officer named Terpas swept the cell with his eyes as he furiously chomped gum, looking rather disappointed that he hadn't caught me misbehaving.

"Take off the turtle suit. Put those on." Terpas tossed orange jail clothes toward me and left. I quickly changed and folded the turtle suit next to me. "C'mon. You've got a video call with Marissa about pre-trial release."

"Okay sir," I said as I got up and followed Terpas to the video phone, just outside the padded cell.

"Sit down and wait." Terpas ordered.

"Yes sir." I said and waited, relieved to be out of the padded cell.

"Micah, can you hear me?" Marissa asked.

"Yes."

"We're going to see if you qualify for pre-trial release. If you do, you'll be getting out of jail today."

"Okay." A tentative hope haphazardly swelled in my chest.

"Since you're a first-time offender, all you need is a place to stay and a job."

"Oh." *Shit*.

"You'll be going to the virtual court room from inside the jail today because of the pandemic."

As Officer Terpas escorted several inmates and me to the jail's improvised courtroom, I kept my head up but my eyes unfocused.

"That's the kid-fucker block," an inmate behind me said as we walked past a cell block with a large P above the door.

"Fucking chomos," another inmate said.

"No talking!" Terpas barked. We walked through a gymnasium and down a hall and arrived at the door of the courtroom. "No talking to the opposite sex!"

I sat and listened to the other inmates whispering, networking, reminiscing and flirting. I kept my eyes on a portly man wearing a suit that hadn't fit him since 15 pounds ago. He was calling inmates into the hall.

"Micah Losh!" the portly man yelled, mispronouncing both names.

I walked out into the hall to speak to the man.

"I'm Jake, I handle all of the pre-trial release cases," he said.

"Hey," I replied nervously.

"All you need to qualify for pre-trial release is a job and an address." Jake held his clipboard with one hand and struggled to pull his pants up with the other.

"I just quit my job of 11 years to stay at home with my sons. I have a home, I live with my family."

"Does he live there?" Jake tapped his finger on Ian's name.

"Yeah."

"There's a no contact order against him so you can't go there." The walls fluttered behind Jake. "What about your parents?"

"My father is dead and I'm dead to my mother."

"Do you have any friends you can call?"

"My best friend and his wife live about twenty minutes away. I could drive to his house, but I don't know his address or his phone number. I have his number saved in my phone, though. His name is Ivan."

"Shit! Alright, I'll do my best."

When I was called before the judge, I sat before a massive monitor and a camera.

"Micah has a friend named Ivan that lives nearby and he just quit a job he'd held for 11 years," Jake pleaded.

I knew Jake was telling the truth, but it sounded like a lie to me. I was an unemployed man, accused of battering and strangling a little boy, and I had a place to go but I didn't know the address or if they'd even have me. *I* wouldn't believe me.

"Mr. Losh – did I say that correctly?" The judge asked.

"No ma'am," I said. "It rhymes with Josh."

"Mr. Losh, you may be the victim of several unfortunate circumstances but unfortunately I cannot approve you for pre-trial release today."

The judge sounded sincere, but it was little comfort.

I spent my first night in an 8-by-12 cell alone with the buzzing overhead light as my only company. Someone had pulled the cord out of the phone, but it didn't matter. My mother's number was the only one I remembered, and I was doubtful she'd take my call. I climbed onto the top bunk, closed my eyes, and tried to will myself to sleep. I sat up to look at the door after I heard a thud against it. I closed my eyes tight and pushed myself against the wall. I heard the thud again.

"Child abuser piece of shit!" Terpas screamed.

"His wife is hot," Wurst said. "Remember when we slammed him onto that gurney?"

"Yeah." Terpas laughed.

"Maybe I'll go and console her," Wurst chortled.

"I'm gonna call the woman with the detection dog," Terpas said cheerfully.

It felt safer to stay awake until the next morning. After breakfast I got my first cellmate, as he slept soundly and I stared at the stains and peeling paint on the ceiling, trying to see different things in them. The window was covered with a thick film, I guessed it to be the afternoon. I heard the thud once more. I looked at my cellmate who was sleeping. *Am I insane?*

"She's on her way. She's hungry, she hasn't been fed all day," Terpas said.

"Let's strap him down naked," Stalwart said. "We'll make him drink our spit and eat bugs."

I heard my mother, Nova, Ivan, Cyrus and Ian, they were there to watch me be punished. I wanted to hold Ian's face and tell him how sorry I was, how much I loved him. I closed my eyes, but it did little to stop the stream of tears.

"Just to clarify, you guys are okay with us hurting him?" Wurst asked.

I strained to hear as my heart drummed in my ears.

"You sure you don't want to stay and watch?" Terpas asked.

Visions of being burnt alive flashed in my head.

"I know what we're gonna do," Stalwart said. "We're gonna call him to shower after dinner and once he's in that far shower room we're going to give him a minute to undress before we open the door and let the dog in. We're gonna give him clothes that smell like weed."

I felt like so many biblical characters that had strayed from Jehovah and suffered so I prayed to Jehovah genuinely and sincerely. I prayed that He would forgive me, that He would help me to save my marriage and to look after my children, for my mother and I to reconnect. I apologized for looking at apostate material, for disrespecting the elders, for not being patient. I told Jehovah I would walk into that room without giving the officers any trouble, that I would be a model prisoner and I pleaded that He would allow me to return to Him. I realized how far I had drifted. I wanted to return to Jehovah. I heard someone unlocking the door and sat up, ready to meet my fate.

"You want a shower?" Officer Tye asked.

"Yes sir," I said. *Is he the one with the dog?*

When I got into the shower room, I smelled the jail clothes. They smelled chemical and awful, but they didn't smell like marijuana. I undressed and climbed into the shower next to a big door. *That's where the dog will enter.* I quickly lathered up and rinsed off. I was confused as I dressed and left the shower room.

"You done already?" Tye asked.

"Yeah." I nodded.

"That was quick! Do you not know how to wash your ass right?"

"I do."

"They fixed the phone in your cell."

"Thank you, sir."

When I logged into the video phone it showed I had one contact, it was Nova. *Thank Jehovah.* When I spoke to Nova she told me Cyrus had been crying for me and that I had left bruises on Ian's chest.

"Did I hit him?" I asked.

"You wouldn't let go of him. You fell on him. It was pretty bad, you really scared him. You really scared me."

"I'm so sorry, my love."

"I put money on here so you can video chat with Cyrus and get a few things."

"Thank you." I hoped she still loved me.

I didn't ask Nova if she had been at the jail, it sounded too crazy to ask and I was somewhat worried she would say she had. I wasn't sure if I was hallucinating, experiencing isolation dementia, or detoxing. I spent a day in an 8-by-12 cell with a man who was detoxing from alcohol. He thought we were hiding in his grandma's garage and saw his family where I saw a wall. The man was about three inches taller than me and easily weighed 80 pounds more than me. In the middle of the night, he slapped my calf while I slept and told me he'd told his grandmother that I was his boyfriend, but she hadn't believed him. He screamed at me to get out of bed before he dragged my ass out, but he didn't touch me again. When he became aggressive with the corrections officers, I was moved into an 8-by-12 with two other inmates in it. One of them had a Bible and I asked him about it.

"I don't want the fucking thing," Daryl said as he tossed me his Bible. "I've just been keeping it under my pillow."

"Are you sure?" I asked.

"Yep. That fucking dumbass that was in here before you left it. He was half a tard, but he read and quoted from the thing all the time."

"Thank you." I said. I felt that Jehovah was reaching out to me, it was comforting. It's possible that the feeling of my God causing something to happen in my life had never been more comforting.

I began voraciously reading that Bible. I read a chapter for each day I had been in jail until I caught up and a new one each day. I made a point to not curse and to be polite to others. I witnessed to multiple cellmates and tried to be long-suffering.

I was in a cell with a man named Clarence who I believe was insane – if he wasn't born mentally ill, he must have smoked enough synthetic marijuana to induce insanity.

Clarence would be up all night singing into the mirror. One night I woke to see him staring at himself in the mirror.

"Blah!" Clarence stuck his tongue out and flipped his eyes back and forth, laughing to himself. Clarence caught me looking at him.

"Yo! I'm just about to sing yo. This is gonna be my hit, make me known in every house!"

"What time is it?"

"Girl! I'll eat it from the outside. Yeah girl, this nasty motherfucker gonna freak you!" Clarence gyrated his hips as he sang. "Girl I'll eat it from the outside!" Clarence looked at me as if he wanted feedback.

"Provocative." I said.

"Yeah player! You get it! I'm going international, worldwide!"

After breakfast that morning Clarence went to take a shower and returned with clumps of feces smeared into his thinning hair. I stared at him, perplexed, until Officer Sarento returned and removed him from the cell.

"Was he acting strange before he left?" Officer Sarento asked.

"Gee, how could you tell?" I replied.

When Clarence came back to the cell, he looked upset.

"You alright?" I asked.

"Nah man," Clarence said. "I was doing my shit to help my hair regrow faster, thicker and they done fucked my shit all up."

"Sorry. Do you want to play cards?" When you have to sleep in a room with crazy, you want to keep crazy friendly.

"Yeah boy. You deal."

After we'd been playing cards for a while Clarence suddenly slid his palm up my thigh and toward my crotch, his fingers brushing my genitals.

"Do you think I'm fem?" Clarence asked seductively.

"I'm married," I said.

"You love your girl, man! I was just trying to get this dick off. Do you want to keep playing cards?"

"Maybe later, I'm going to draw some more for my son."

My first instinct had been to hit Clarence. I considered waiting for Clarence to fall asleep. He was skinny with a big Adam's apple and I figured if I jumped and landed on his neck, he'd be too busy gasping for air to fight back. I was not going to be raped in jail and I figured I could handle the restraint chair and going to segregation. What if Jehovah was testing me? I had to be peaceable if I was going to serve Jehovah. I wrote my mother a letter and told her I had a problem with alcohol, asked her to have the elders contact me and send me a Bible. I asked her to forgive me. I asked her how she could not care that her only child was in jail and terrified.

After 31 days in 8-by-12 cells I was told I would be moving to a cell block. I gathered up my possessions, including my ripped mattress.

"Sir, which block am I going to?" I asked.

"You find out when you get there," Officer Wurst said.

I'd been to Daxton's office to talk several times. I wondered if he was trying to look out for me since I had never been in jail. He'd told me that I would probably be moving into a small, open block for first time offenders. When the guard stopped walking in front of P block it felt like something collapsed on my lungs.

"Isn't this the block for child molesters?" I asked.

"It's where you're going. C'mon!" Wurst ordered.

The door buzzed open and I followed Wurst inside. As I walked toward my bunk I heard one man ask who I was and another respond that I wasn't shit. I was simultaneously relieved and disappointed to be one of the biggest people in P block. After Wurst left, a group of men gathered behind a small man who was smiling at me with his remaining teeth. He looked like a snake. I closed my eyes. *Please, Jehovah.*

"What's your name?" the small man asked. He had almost as many teeth as he had face tattoos.

"Micah," I said.

"Whassup? I'm Dillon! You fuck kids?" His movements were almost spastic, frenetic energy seemed to emanate from him.

"No," I said flatly.

"We all do! This is the chomo block!" Dillon licked his dry lips as he spread his arms. A lanky man with an underbite yelled he was locked up for barnyard sodomy.

"That's great," I said as my hands shook with anger. *Do I let them all beat me up or do I fight back?*

"I'm just fucking with you!" Dillon jumped up and down as he laughed. "This is the medical block but it's for people in protective custody too. What you in for?"

"I was in a blackout and I attacked my step-son."

"That it?"

"Yeah," I was horrified to say it out loud.

"Shit. We all beat our bitches! You cool!"

"Okay," I said, nonplussed.

"Yo dawg, I just want to know who I'm doing time with." Dillon held his fist out for me to bump.

"I understand." I bumped Dillon's fist with mine.

"Come on back to my house," Dillon said as he gestured behind him. "We'll sit on my front porch!"

"Alright," I said begrudgingly.

"My bitch puts a hundred on my books every week!" Dillon spread his arms back towards his possessions.

"That's nice of her."

"She knows I'll fuck her bitch ass up if she don't! She'll suck dick if she has to!"

"I'm gonna go draw a picture for my son."

"Drawing your jail hustle?"

"No, I've never been in jail before."

"Where ya been?"

"Mostly I was being a Jehovah's Witness."

"I'm real sorry to hear that," Dillon said sincerely. "I had a friend that grew up a Jehovah."

"Oh. Why are you sorry?"

"Cause he was fucked up!" Dillon said as he began drawing. "I fuck with the Bible though. You like meth?"

"I just drink. Drank."

"I love meth! You want to see my bitch? She's a slut! She loves the cock."

"Sure." *Not at all.*

"That hot rod in the pictures, I ate her pussy in the backseat of that car while another bitch drove from Indy to Los Angeles!"

"It's a nice car."

"You got a bitch?"

"I have a wife." I smiled as I thought of Nova. "She's beautiful."

"Yeah! She gonna send you nudes?"

"I doubt it. I made a huge mistake. There was no intention, it could just as easily have been my two-year-old or her."

"You would drown your step-son to save your son," Dillon said as he smiled perversely.

"That's not true." I said weakly.

"Losh!" Officer Sarento yelled.

"Coming!" I went to the front of the block.

"It's a no contact order."

"Okay." I said quietly.

I was confused, it was my mother's name on the paperwork. The no contact order said I had a history of depression, suicidal ideation, that my mother had tried to get me help, that I had threatened to commit suicide by cop, that she worried I'd be angry whenever I was released and she worried for the safety of Ian and Cyrus.

"You need to sign it."

"Sorry," I said as I signed the paperwork.

"You'll go to virtual court for this next week."

"I don't have to wonder if she got my letter anymore," I said as I forced a smile.

Physically Out, Mentally Out

Huddled masses, amassed at mass. Crowded gluttons, a narrow path.
Muddled incantation. Complete disintegration.
This is my waste, what was my faith.
Sycophant. My God I can't.
Swing from rafters, burnt with straw. Hanging worth on capricious laws.
My waste.
My faith.
Sycophant. God I can't.
Obsequious and vicious. Volatile and possible. Son, I'm not a prodigal.
This waste, this faith.
Sycophant.
No I can't. Know I can't.

"Your own mother filed a no contact on you?" Dillon asked.

"Yeah," I said.

"That's fucked! Odin! Dawg, come here!"

"What's up?" Odin asked. The words were muffled by his underbite.

"This motherfucker's own *mother* filed a no contact against him."

"She why you in jail?"

"No, she wasn't there. I wrote her two letters," I said.

"You threaten her?" Odin asked.

"No. I apologized. I asked for help from people in our religion and for a Bible."

"Man, *fuck* that bitch! I've got a friend with HIV. He'll rape any motherfucker you want for $500."

"Thanks," I said. "That's sweet of you."

"Who's your lawyer?"

"A public defender. Phillip Fout, I believe."

"Dawg! You got Fout?"

"Yeah, is that bad?"

"Yo Dillon, he got Fout!"

"Fuck that motherfucker!" Dillon shrieked. "Fout will sell you out!"

"That doesn't bode well," I said.

"He's a buckethead bitch but he's still your lawyer," Odin said. "When you go to court you tell the judge to file a no contact on *her* bitch ass!"

"I probably won't do that, I'm just glad it wasn't my wife."

"Right. Keep my friend in mind, he's always looking for work." Odin smiled as his tongue slid between his teeth.

Officer Sarento escorted me to a different room for virtual court regarding my mother's no contact order. I heard my mother's voice as she stated her name. I floated up out of myself, away from her voice.

It was a Thursday night and my mother hadn't gone to meeting because I hadn't gone to meeting. I was weeks away from turning 21. I was trying to communicate to my mom that the pain was so intense I just wanted to escape it. I didn't want to die, I just wanted the agony to stop. I told my mom that something was wrong and I didn't know what it was. I told my mom that I had a thought about pointing a fake gun at a cop so they would shoot me.

"Mr. Losh?" Judge Rapner said. "Mr. Losh! Are you with us?"

"Yes, your honor. I'm sorry."

"You are to have no contact with your mother," Judge Rapner said loudly. "Do you understand that?" His high-definition, prissy face stared at me.

"Yeah," I said, grinning into the camera. "I have no issue never speaking to her again."

I understood no contact better than Judge Rapner knew. As I walked back to P block, I felt the tears trembling in my eyes.

"Are you doing okay?" Sarento asked.

"Sixteen years. My own mother thinks I would harm my children while I'm sober. Once she found me surrounded by empty beer bottles with a loaded shotgun in my mouth and *left*."

"So you prove her wrong. My parents were addicts and terribly abusive. You get sober for those boys."

God damn right, I thought. Her encouragement was overwhelming to me.

While I waited for P block to buzz me in, I saw Dillon through the glass, looking at me.

"Josh Losh! How'd court go?" Dillon called me by my jail name.

"As good as it gets," I said. "Have you been able to get hold of your sister that works at the treatment facility?"

"Not yet but I will. It's fucked up they said you've been sober too long!"

"Over thirty days is too long, evidently."

"You want me to buy you some hand sanitizer on commissary? You can eat that shit and tell them you relapsed."

"No."

"What's your bitch ass lawyer been doing for you?"

"It's difficult to catch him. He's probably busy drinking prune juice."

"That motherfucker is fucking old."

"He told me that the prosecutor wanted Ian to testify, but I don't want to traumatize him more. My wife doesn't want him to do it either."

I sat down on my bunk which faced the glass in the hallway. Inmates walked past and one of them mouthed 'chomo.'

"So what're you gonna do?"

"If I sign a plea bargain, will the no contact order be lifted?"

"Should be. You sign that shit and they lift it! Make sure Fout don't sell you out!"

"I'll do my best."

I tried to hang myself that night. Odin had taught me how to make two small holes in a towel and hang it from exposed screws to shield the hallway's light. I hung my shirt and a towel to block the hallway and camera as best I could. I fashioned a noose out of my long sleeve thermal shirt I had bought from commissary. I tied the best knot I could, got on my knees, and leaned as hard as I could, trying to make myself pass out, but I couldn't make it work. *You really suck at killing yourself.* I didn't know if God was real or not, but I hated Him. I laid in my bunk wide awake until they brought P block breakfast. After I ate, I called my lawyer.

"How're you doing?" Fout asked chipperly.

"I'm alright," I said. "Neither my wife nor I want to further traumatize my step-son. If I sign the plea bargain will the no contact order be lifted?"

"That's the way it usually works," Fout said. "Call me next week."

Isolation and independent thought had been discouraged my entire life. It was difficult to isolate in jail, but I did my best to think. I only had myself to rely on. When one inmate touched my shoulder and assured me not to be afraid of him, I scoffed, and then I told him if he touched me again, I'd stab him in his femoral artery while he slept. I asked him if he knew how quickly his body would pump blood out of him. When officers interrogated me about if I had any knowledge of jail tattoos, I lied straight to their faces and told them I hadn't seen anything. When Officer Wurst called me "Lush," I told him to suck a syphilitic cock as he left for the day. I told Dillon I hated another inmate named Blessing.

"Blessing is a delusional fuckhead." I said. "He said he shouldn't have to pay his back-child support once they're 18. He needs to stop having kids, he has *nine*."

"What is your problem?" Dillon asked me. He was inches from my face.

"What do you mean?" I asked.

"You ain't no better than Blessing's dumb ass! You're a child strangler. You could be looking at five years inside!"

"Maybe, but I didn't intentionally break the law. He intentionally neglects his children."

"You don't have anywhere to go do you? You can stay here or go to seg. Make a move nigga!" Dillon stared at me.

I stared at Dillon; I wanted him to hit me. Dillon gave Blessing food after he chewed up a toenail, gave him coffee when he was tired on the condition that he chewed the grounds. I wanted to tell Dillon that it was fucking idiotic how a bunch of racist peckerwoods appropriated racial epithets. I wanted to tell Dillon that just because he kept coming back to jail didn't mean he had mastered it. I wanted to tell Dillon that Daxton had told me that there were no gangstas in P block, including him. I stared at Dillon wondering if he was going to hit me. I turned my head away, making sure not to look down.

"You good?" Dillon said as he held out his fist.

"Yeah," I said as I looked at Dillon with hatred. I bumped his fist halfheartedly.

"Good, I got a job for you."

"What's that?"

"My boy wants to get praying hands tattooed on him, I want you to draw them."

"You can draw better than me."

"I'm too busy. I'll pay you."

"Sure."

I spent the rest of the week drawing my hands praying. Once, I was finished I gave the picture to Dillon and he tattooed my hands on another inmate's shoulder. Dillon paid me in food. *Drawing is my jail hustle.*

The following week I called my public defender. I missed praying to Jehovah, feeling like He cared about me.

"Good news – your plea bargain has come in!" Fout exclaimed.

"What does it offer?" I asked.

"Well why don't I send this over to you before your court date on Monday?"

"Okay."

That night as I laid in my bunk, I stared up at the picture I'd drawn of Nova. It fell and hit me in the face. *Some people might interpret this as a sign.* The picture was torn from when a corrections officer had ripped it down during a shakedown. *I love you Nova.* I tried not to think about if any pedophiles had looked at Cyrus when I video chatted with him. I played cards with one man accused of statutory rape and pedophilia and another who plead guilty to 10 counts of child pornography. They both said they were innocent, and they were both believable. My plea bargain never arrived, and my mind wouldn't shut off.

Monday arrived. After breakfast Stalwart came to bring me to court, I was worried because the plea bargain still hadn't come. We walked to the gymnasium and the door buzzed open, it was filled with inmates. A room full of prisoners and I could feel every single one of their eyes on me.

"You fuck them kids?" An inmate yelled. The gym filled with frenzied screams.

"Shut the fuck up!" Stalwart yelled. "All of you!"

Outside of the courtroom, I heard Judge Rapner talking.

"Mr. Channard, you are on probation, is that right?" Judge Rapner asked.

"Yes sir, I caught a case for crack cocaine and was on probation," Channard answered.

"To begin with, we don't *catch* cases in this county! We are charged. Do you understand?"

"Yes sir."

"Secondly, did you really believe you could use methamphetamine while on probation?"

"I only got in trouble for coke."

Their arguing began to sound distant as I retreated into my mind. That morning I'd separated my possessions into three piles, what I'd give away, what I'd throw away, and what I'd keep. I asked myself where the plea bargain was, I resented a God I didn't believe in, and I missed my family.

"Is Mr. Losh here?" Judge Rapner asked.

"Yes," I said as I popped up.

"You are going to trial? Is that correct?"

"No. I was told last Wednesday that there was a plea bargain and I was waiting to receive it."

"Mr Fout, is that true?"

"Not that I'm aware of," Fout said.

"We will see you at trial," Rapner said.

As Stalwart walked me through the gymnasium another inmate screamed, asking me if I preferred little boys or girls. I wanted them to swarm, beat me to death.

"Sorry about that," Stalwart said as P block buzzed open.

I didn't know if Stalwart meant the other inmates or what happened in court, and I didn't care. I sat on my bunk and went to a place behind my corneas, the volume of reality turned down to an indecipherable hum. When I realized Stalwart was yelling my name, my consciousness lurched up – I came with it, realizing I had stood upright – and all of a sudden, my vision came back.

"Losh!" Stalwart yelled.

"What?" I asked.

"They want you back in court."

Back in the courtroom, my plea bargain was placed onto my lap. It said I would be on probation for 18 months, but it didn't say anything about the no contact order being lifted. The inclination to say a quick prayer surfaced. *You don't do that shit anymore.* I tried to imagine sleeping in my car and staying close to Cyrus. My head filled with images of meth heads, pedophiles and how so many inmates in P block would swing their genitals at me and say "Look at my dick. Queer!" I signed the plea bargain. I'd rather live outdoors and still see Cyrus than stay in jail. I had to say that I "applied pressure" to Ian's throat for the court. The words were the distant speech of a stranger.

"Kill yourself," Channard suggested as I walked past him. I smirked as Stalwart rebuked Channard. *Maybe I will.*

As I gathered my things, I stole a book from jail. The book was the first in the *Witcher* series. I had spent hours playing the game while Ian watched. I would have liked to have believed it was a sign, but I felt it was only a coincidence. Terpas came to the door and told me, "Time to go."

"I want you to look me up on social media!" Dillon said.

"I will," I lied as I walked out of P block. *I don't ever want to see any of you again.*

I had been in jail for 77 days, but it might as well have been 77 years. I walked out of jail 14 pounds lighter. I ran towards the home I could no longer live in; towards the family I could no longer live with. After I knocked, Nova opened the door. *She's so beautiful.* I rushed to hug her. When I smelled her hair my legs buckled.

"I'm sorry," I said.

"I was sleeping," Nova said.

"I'm sorry. Where is my car? I have to go to probation today."

"Your car was repossessed."

"Why didn't you tell me?"

"I don't know." Nova shrugged.

"Can I take your car?"

"Just be back so I have time to get to work. You can sleep here tonight."

"Okay." I made a face as a weather alert went off on my phone. "How do I have service?" I asked.

"Your mom said it wouldn't save her much to remove you from the bill, so she'll just pay for it."

"She doesn't care if I'm homeless, but she's worried about how many *bars* I'll have?"

"I don't know, I need to sleep."

After Nova left, I apologized to Ian's empty room. *I went from a Jehovah's Witness to a violent felon on probation with two no contact orders.* I was a ghost haunting my former life. I sent a former co-worker named Scarlotte a message that I was out, it was cold, and I was homeless. When Scarlotte asked what I was going to do I told her that I didn't know and that I wanted to jump off of a bridge. She and her husband Dale had moved to Florida before I went to jail. I flopped back, exhausted, and closed my eyes. I sat up when I heard a knock. *Who the fuck is that?* It had to be either the elders or someone related to Ian. They knocked again and I got on the ground. My phone started to ring, and I quickly answered to quiet it.

"Hello," I answered.

"Where are you?" Dale asked.

"Why?"

"Tell me where you are!"

"Tell me why you want to know."

"We've called the police!"

"What? Why?"

"To check on you! You said you were going to jump off of a bridge."

"Fuck! I'm on probation."

"You'll be fine. You haven't done anything wrong. Where are you?"

"In the woods," I lied. "I got lost out here."

I hung up and put my head against the floor. I heard the police knocking again. I didn't know what to do, so I opened the door.

"I'm Officer Owens. Is Micah here?"

"Yeah, I'm becoming quite notorious," I said.

"Can I see your phone?" Owens asked.

"Yeah."

"We need you to come with us. You've made a threat against your life."

"A threat against my life? 'I want to jump off a bridge is an expression."

"You need to be evaluated at the hospital."

"I've been in jail for 77 days. I just want to see my son. I'm supposed to see him tomorrow. His name is Cyrus. Please don't deny me that!"

"Then you shouldn't have shown me your phone!"

"I'm on probation, I thought I had to do whatever you asked."

"Sir, you're coming with us."

"Can I put some underwear and real pants on? I'm in pajamas."

"No. You need to come with us now."

"God damn it! All this because of some moron in Florida."

"I need to handcuff you."

"Of course you do. If I tell someone to jump in a lake, is that attempted murder?"

As he walked me down the stairs a light flipped on in a window. The silhouette of a little boy watched me as I climbed into the back of a police car in pajamas and house shoes. *Monsters are real, kid.* I writhed against the discomfort of the handcuffs in the back of the cruiser. Owens pulled off and the closer we got to the hospital, the angrier I became.

"Do you ever wonder why people hate the police?" I asked.

"I'm not trying to do anything to you."

"You are, whether or not you intend to. You're keeping me from my little boy."

"Tell them the truth at the hospital."

"I told you the truth, did that do me any good? You're actively causing harm in my life."

"I'm just doing my job."

"I believe Nazis said something similar." *Fuck you. Fuck Scarlotte. Fuck God! Fuck me.*

When Owens pulled up to the curb at the hospital, he allowed me to call Nova to briefly explain what was going on. A nurse and a security guard approached us. The nurse cheerfully told me her name was Staci.

"How're you doing today?" Staci asked.

"Fed up to the teeth with rhetorical questions," I said. "I just got out of jail, I'm a violent felon, homeless, jobless, no car and I have no money to pay for this. I was supposed to see my son tomorrow but a dumb fuck in Florida called the police on me because I said I should jump off a bridge."

"You're going to go with them." Owens said as he removed the handcuffs.

"You're leaving already?" I asked as I rubbed my wrists. The security guard grasped his belt buckle as if to assert himself. "I go with rent-a-cop, huh? Text me when you get there so I know you're safe!"

I was taken into a room and told I needed to put on a blue jumpsuit made of paper. The crotch ripped out of it as I sat down. I told everyone how badly I wanted to see Cyrus the next day, which proved I didn't have a suicide plan. I stared at the ceiling in the room I was locked in for nearly ten hours; it reminded me of the ceilings in the 8-by-12 cells. I sat in anxiety, anger, and hatred, and although I missed praying and feeling Jehovah was concerned for me, I refused to do it. When I saw paramedics through the glass door, I knew they were going to take me to a stress center. A woman with a nice smile asked if I could climb on the gurney for them.

"Yeah." I said. "Let's get this shit over with." Rent-a-cop was staring at me, so I flipped off the blanket and splayed my legs. *Get a good look, asshole.* Rent-a-cop followed us down the hall and watched as the paramedics loaded me into the back of the ambulance. He told me not to give the girls any trouble.

"Thanks dad!" I screamed as I gave him two enthusiastic thumbs up. "When's the last time you saw your junk, fat-ass? I bet it was before Obama. Choke on a prolapsed anus! Bitch!"

The paramedics laughed as they slid me into the back of the ambulance and out of his sight. The paramedic with the nice smile hopped in the back with me and asked if I was going to give her any trouble.

"No," I said softly. "I just want my son."

The paramedic smiled at me and assured me they would get me back to Cyrus.

"I wish," I said. "Allow me to regale you with how utterly fucked I am."

When the ambulance arrived at the hospital, an RN in glasses took me to into a room and told me I needed to put on a gown. He offered to turn around.

"Those glasses don't make you look any smarter," I said. "I lost my modesty in jail. Feel free to take it in."

The medical staff listened to my situation and forced me to take a sleeping pill. I was worried it would be a violation of my probation, since I couldn't take any controlled substance or even use CBD. The next day, after contacting Nova to corroborate my story, the hospital paid for a ride to take me back to where I was homeless. I got out of the car and shivered in the cold wind, then began walking to stay warm.

Nova told me that day that Ivan had said that I couldn't stay with him and his wife because of Jehovah's standards about an unmarried man and a woman being together. Ivan was working nights now. I left desperate, pleading voicemails on a few Jehovah's Witnesses' phones and they all went unanswered. Co-workers refused me shelter for *one* night. I would have slept in garages, sheds or next to livestock. A coworker told me to go and get a job and to be thankful I wasn't being judged. *As a Christian, you aren't allowed to judge me anyway.* A friend named Brooke, who I always thought was a kind and beautiful person, offered to bring me some blankets and gave me $80. After we caught up, I went into a drugstore and used the bathroom, then walked down the road to buy a hamburger.

After I ate, I called or walked to every local shelter I could find, but none of them were able to help me or I didn't fit their stipulations. I walked all over my town before I found myself near a bridge and crawled underneath it. It was louder than I expected, and it shook when cars drove over it. Massive cobwebs indicated massive spiders – or very industrious ones. I sussed out where I could sleep and be bitten the least. *Is this my life now? I want to get drunk.* I had money in my pocket, and I was near a liquor store I used to frequent. Nobody would know. I didn't like who I had become. I hated what I did to Ian and it could have just as easily been Cyrus. You can drink, I thought, but you can't drink and say you love those boys. I felt a fear so gargantuan it made me question if I'd ever truly experienced the emotion before. I walked back to the drugstore I'd gone to earlier. After I used the restroom, an employee was waiting for me and asked me to leave.

"I'm really sorry," I said, humiliated.

I headed toward the apartment to meet Nova – she had told me I could sleep in her car that night. I stood across the street from my family watching Nova get the boys out of her car. I was an unseen, stalking monster to a child that feared me. I whispered Ian's name, afraid he might hear me. It ached to see how happy they were without me. *I'll do whatever you want, I just wish you didn't want me to go away.*

Nova brought down blankets and pillows. I'd hoped they'd smell more like her than they did. In the morning I would call halfway houses.

"Mercy House! How may I help you?" A woman's voice answered my call the following morning.

"Hi," I said softly. "My name is Micah." I explained my situation and held my breath.

"Hi Micah. I'm Jo. You are welcome to come down today so we can discuss things."

"Thank you," I said, relieved. "My wife will drive me down later today."

I packed my bags and waited for Nova. When Cyrus saw me, he was frightened at first. Perhaps he remembered the night I went to jail. I loaded up my luggage and we headed to Mercy House. I analyzed Cyrus' facial structure in the car; he'd changed so much since I'd been away. Cyrus looked at me adoringly and I looked away so he wouldn't see the agony twitching in my face.

"If I don't get into this place, can you drive me to the homeless shelter?" I asked.

"What do you mean if?" Nova asked.

"This isn't guaranteed," I said. "The woman I spoke to said she would interview me, I guess."

"I really can't. I have to pick up Ian."

"I understand," I said.

When we arrived, I told Cyrus and Nova that I loved them. I couldn't stomach watching Nova drive off. I looked up the stairs at Mercy House, wishing I would disassociate. To the right of the house, in an attached yard, a group of men were seated in a circle, their speech indistinct. I carried my luggage up the stairs and into Mercy House. Inside, there was an office to the right, opposite the stairs.

"Can I help you?" the woman seated at the desk asked.

"Hi," I said. "I'm Micah, I believe we spoke this morning. Are you Jo?"

"Yes."

Jo smiled with her mouth, but her eyes darted at my luggage. She crossed her arms across her breasts, pushing together her slightly wrinkled cleavage. Jo was in her late 50s. She wore black rimmed glasses, her face was framed by dyed black hair, and the lines in her face had been carved deeply by years of alcohol and cocaine. Her fingers ended in black gel nails.

"I'm not trying to force your hand or anything," I said. "If I don't get in here, I'll walk to the shelter."

"Why don't you go out to the fire pit meeting and we'll talk afterward?"

"Okay," I said.

Programming

Wading out of a shadow and breeding contempt.
A familiarity for which I have no fondness in the deafening absence.
Between a precursor to indiscretion and the smallest breach after your mind opens.
A pomegranate floating beauty.
Were you the only thing I loved or did I love you because you were the only thing?
Am I so desperate to be different or is what I am so desperate?
Imbuing granite garnet.
A mind of clandestine sedition.
Loneliness within my isolation.
Immortality flees.
Truest in pain.
Without idioms to suffer or isms to swallow.

Approaching the meeting, I was met with a great fall oak of a man in mid speech. Tall, broad, with a thinning crown of red hair, his strikingly soft voice rumbled out from under his Fu Manchu mustache. "What's up, brother?" His eyes had a cautiously friendly, energetic aspect.

"May I sit down?" I asked. I didn't want to interrupt, but the group had interrupted itself to observe my approach.

"Yeah man, what's your name? I'm Umber." He kept his eyes half lidded, but his demeanor and character seemed well intentioned.

"Micah," I said.

"Do you want a cigarette?" Umber asked.

I politely declined. Their eyes lingered on me for a second longer – far longer than I would have liked – before Umber resumed the interrupted discussion, on a former resident's relapse, and on whether snitches deserved stitches. I didn't care about the relapse. I didn't care *if I cared* about the relapse – I had already spent more than enough time trying to save people. Self-preservation and getting back to my family were the only things on my mind. As the meeting dragged on, the light faded and the cold crept in. The fear I'd felt contemplating sleeping under the bridge resurfaced. Walking back into Jo's office, my thoughts were a train of the repeated phrase "learn to swim." Jo smiled and asked what I had thought of my first meeting.

"Uh...it was good," I said. "I want be sober, so I want to be around people that are trying to get sober."

A brief pause. "What are you willing to do to get sober?"

"I won't drink," I said. Another lingering pause. It seemed like she was prompting me for a specific phrase, but I had no idea what she was anticipating.

"It's about being *honest*, having an *open mind*, and being *willing*." Her tone was one of a kindergarten teacher reminding children that they have to be nice and share with one another. This fixation on specific wording and phrases would reassert itself throughout my stay, another unfortunate reminder of my time as a Jehovah's Witness.

"Okay." I nodded quickly. *Please just tell me if I can stay.*

Jo blinked and assumed a business-as-usual voice. "Can you pass a drug test?"

"Of course." I bounced my leg nervously. *What if I ate something with poppy seeds in it?*

"If you pass it, we'll talk more."

Umber took me into a bathroom and gave me a cup. "Piss in that," he said. I turned on the faucet and drank several cups of water before I could urinate. Umber's strange, soft voice did not help my endeavors. When my urine came back clear, Jo looked surprised.

"I thought you were on meth," Jo said. She almost sounded disappointed. "We'll try you out for the weekend at first. See how that goes."

"Thank you!" I gushed.

"There's just something about you that I don't trust." *Okay?* "You're going to have to follow the rules here." I felt a little stung, to be regarded so suspiciously in a place for addicts, but I was mostly thrilled to not be spending the night as a homeless man.

"I won't be a problem."

"Umber is going to go through your luggage." I nodded, and Umber began doing just that.

"Here at Mercy House you aren't allowed to work for the first five weeks, so you can adjust to sobriety. You'll need to surrender your wallet, keys phone, and any money you may have." Jo's tone had switched from kindergarten teacher to warden in a second.

"Of course." I pulled my wallet and phone out of my pocket, I sighed as I looked at the picture of Nova on my phone before I turned it off. I said, "My car was repossessed while I was in jail." I laid my wallet and phone on Jo's desk.

"Any phone calls you make must be supervised. No hos."

"I'm married."

"You're allowed to speak to your wife, but it must be supervised."

"That's fine."

Jo held up my wallet and exclaimed, "You've got money in here!" This was the first time she had registered sincere surprise, breaking the world-weary intake woman character for a second.

"Yeah, I do."

"What kind of addict shows up at a halfway house with sixty-three dollars?" Jo chuckled as she put the bills in an envelope and wrote my name on it.

"Brooke gave it to me."

"Is she your side bitch?"

"What? No. We worked together for eleven years." *What kind of questions are these?*

"What kind of addict shows up at a halfway house with cash and matching luggage?" Umber asked, chuckling as well.

"I don't know," I said. "I've had this luggage a long time. Don't most adults?"

"I never did," Jo said.

"You can't have this mouthwash," Umber said as he held up my cologne. "You're not drinking this, are you?"

"No. I would never drink cologne." My response was terse, but I was a little annoyed at the suggestion.

"A real addict would," Jo said.

"I'm not an addict, I drank a lot. I was allowed to drink."

"You need to stop looking at what's different and start looking at what's the same. If you're on any meds they need to stay in the office." Another cliché to paper over any point of potential disagreement.

"Okay." *You're the one who brought up the difference between me and a "real addict".* "What if I bought vitamins?"

"No. People have been known to take a bunch to see if they can get anything off of them."

"That's crazy."

"It's a disease. You'll be in stage one for the first five weeks; if you move into stage two, you'll receive more privileges like getting your phone back and being able to leave by yourself." Jo slid a paper toward me. "Sign here," she said with a smile.

The highly structured days, scheduled meetings, and forced socializing felt eerily familiar. I was assigned a mentor to help me acclimate to Mercy House, a pudgy Puerto Rican named Hector who quoted gangster movies a lot. He gave me a tour of the property, showed me how to do my chores, and told me about smoking synthetic marijuana, being homeless, and how he had slept in a plastic slide at a park and gotten mugged. I liked Hector. When I saw him visiting with his two young daughters, I watched their faces light up as their father knelt to hug them.

Hector was scheduled to move into stage two a week after my arrival, but he wanted it to be moved up so he could look at pornography. Jo wanted Hector to wait an additional week, so he took his phone and left. I was flabbergasted and I tried not to think about how happy his daughters had been. I discovered that day that it was customary to discuss a departed resident.

"Okay guys, quiet down." Jo sighed as she leaned against the wall in a dark blue dress. She stared at a man in camouflage named Dale until he looked up.

"What?" Dale asked in a Southern drawl.

"I need you to quit coloring and listen."

"I can color and listen, Jo," Dale objected.

"I am always transparent with you guys, and I expect your full attention." Expert schoolmarm voice.

"Speaking of transparency, I want to know who stole my cheese!" Dale craned his pudgy neck and head around to sweep the rest of the circle.

"Dale, what are you talking about?"

"I was counting my cheese slices earlier and I'm one short. I thought we were supposed to be brothers." It was easy to think lightly of the matter, but the genuine sting in his voice gave it delicious ridiculous pathos.

"People shouldn't be stealing, but is it possible you miscounted?"

Dale demurred for a second, then stood up and muttered, "I'll go recount."

"You can count your cheese later." Exasperation was creeping into Jo's voice.

A heavily tattooed man in a sleeveless shirt named Clayton pounded the table and said, "Bro, put your ass crack away!"

"Fuck you!" Dale said.

"Hector left today!" Jo yelled. "That is what we are here to discuss." I groaned as I pushed my brow into my hand. Taking note, Jo asked, "Micah, why do you think he left?"

"Why are you asking me?" I asked.

"You're new here, I'm curious what your perspective is."

"Hector quoted mobster movies a lot and he chose pornography over living inside," I said as I shifted in my chair. I wasn't trying to besmirch his character, but I wasn't willing to lie about his behavior either.

"Like you don't have naked pictures of your wife on your phone? He wasn't willing." Another voice from the group chimed in, dumping yet another cliché on the ground.

"He wasn't thinking clearly, he's possibly mentally ill. He was sober. Why was him leaving the kinder, better option," I asked.

"You gotta be willing, yo!" Clayton said as he spread his sleeveless arms. Again, this blind obedience to the slogans and phrases that shaped our views of ourselves and recovery. A loud clatter interrupted, and everyone looked over to see Hector stumbling into Mercy House. "What the fuck, bro?" Clayton said.

"What are you doing here, Hector?" Jo spoke softly, but firmly. "You're not allowed for two months, we discussed this."

Hector mumbled about how he appreciated being put on the path to sobriety, his eyes shining from the influence of something or other. He had hugged his daughters almost exactly where he stood, their eyes had shined from tears. I had to look away. Jo escorted Hector outside and came back in with a solemn look on her face.

"Hector admitted something to me outside," Jo said. "Several weeks ago, he asked a girl to meet him out back by the dumpster for sex."

"Yeah bro!" Clayton cheered.

"This is serious! This is why I tell you guys not to speak to women."

"I was just clowning Jo. You right."

A man wearing a Confederate flag ring named Bud said, "Sometimes they want it just as bad as us!" Bud had previously told me that he didn't get why "the blacks," had a problem with his ring.

"Yo!" A 450 pound man in a track suit named Dallas called out. "It's like, yeah dawg. I know I just got to Mercy and all, but I appreciate it, yo. When my granny packed me up to come here, she told me follow the rules and I feel like she was right. So even if a shorty wants to holla, we ain't got to do that no more!" Dallas talked about how his cock was like a horse's and when he'd do meth next outside of meetings.

"Okay guys, it's almost lunch," Jo said. "Let's recover, gentlemen!"

"Thank God that's over," I said, as the group started to disperse.

"What's wrong, player?" Dallas asked.

"What's wrong is how am I actually in a room full of adults being instructed not to have sex by a dumpster." I felt like I was drowning in my own compounded misery.

"You don't want to be judgmental though."

I snorted. "Did you ever think that maybe failing to practice judgement is the biggest problem around here?"

"You think you're better than us?" Clayton asked as he spread his arms.

"It's not about that. This is a waste of my time, I don't need to be told not to fornicate by the dumpster! I don't project attacking a child onto others, because I was the one who did that."

"You've never picked up a bitch from a meeting before?" Dallas asked.

"No, I'm married. I never dated a meth whore," I replied.

"Guys!" Clayton shouted. "Let's just all not focus on bitches right now. Yeah, I got bitches sending me titties and ass, but it ain't good for me right now!"

I walked to the coffee pot and poured myself a cup. I grimaced as I remembered telling Nova I took my coffee "like a basic white bitch." I missed her gorgeous laugh and how it showed all of her teeth.

"Yo player," Dallas said. "Jo needs you in the office."

"Nothing would bring me more pleasure," I said flatly.

"You good bro?"

"It's strenuous to be popular." I smiled as I stirred my coffee. Regrettably, I could feel myself starting to take out my frustration in responses to innocuous questions.

"You got a shit eating grin man, for real."

"Yeah? I used to be a pretty funny guy." I pointedly stirred my coffee and walked to Jo's office.

"You wanted to see me?" I asked.

"Shut the door," Jo said. I pushed it shut as I took a sip of coffee.

"Why did you feel it was necessary to mention meth?" Jo asked sternly.

"Well, it wasn't that I felt it was necessary. This is where people's priorities are? I take this seriously." I could hear a defensive edge in my voice, but I couldn't stop myself from reinforcing it.

"And you feel they don't?"

"Some of them certainly don't. I hear them on the porch or away from the meetings. I made an assumption when I said meth. I just figured that if you're going to copulate next to that filthy dumpster, you're probably partial to meth." God, it felt good to vent. The more this place reminded me of being a Jehovah's Witness, the more frustrated I found myself, the more internal strife I found when trying to adhere to a strict, unquestioned psychic path.

Jo pursed her lips. "You need to meet people where they are at."

"Do you mean by the dumpster? This is serious."

"Did you ever think that you could help them?" Again, that condescending tone.

"I need to focus on myself. Look-" I adjusted in my chair "-I don't actively wish most of these guys harm, but I don't care if they do drugs either. My *family* is my focus. I attacked Ian. It's important to me to get this right. I have nothing in common with them."

"You need to meet them where they're at." Again, that stupid cliché! Is that all that Jo had to offer me?

"Fuck them where they're at! Sorry I don't want to spend time with people that would have sex by a dumpster. I don't like people that refer to women as bitches either."

"You're so desperate to be different." Despite my own obvious antipathy towards this conversation, this was a point where I really felt that Jo showed some of the same, for her part as well. Evaluating me as an individual at this point, instead of treating me as the latest in a long string of functionally and morally equivalent addict, would have made all the difference in the world. But here she was, just like the elders. One solution to the world's problems.

"I wasn't shooting up with pond water, I wasn't pimping out my girlfriend, I wasn't intentionally breaking the law. Did you know one of them told me that they gathered up the bedbugs that had bitten them, smashed them up and chewed them because bedbugs don't digest meth?"

"You could try meth if you drank again."

"Smoking meth is insane. I would never do that." I was getting audibly frustrated with this conversation.

"You don't know everything."

"I never once claimed to possess all of the world's knowledge. I just want to try to help my family. I'm afraid my mother will try to convert my family and then they'll shun me!"

"You can't control everything." The petulance in her voice was driving me to wrath.

"I never said I could. I just feel that I have to try."

"Feelings aren't facts."

"Facts are facts. Millions of people have been told that people like me serve Satan. I know because I was raised that way and I believed it when they said it about other people. I know how crazy I sound."

"We don't see the world as it is, we see it as we are." At this point, I was exhausted with trying to have a real conversation with an endless hedge maze of recovery clichés.

"If that's true of me, isn't it true of you too? Seems a little capricious."

"Do you use big words to elevate yourself?"

"There are no big words, there are long words," I said. "If the way I speak makes you feel inferior, that's a commentary on you."

It was her turn to purse her lips and get frustrated. "You'll get it. You need a sponsor, so I found you one. His name is Nicholas. Go recover!"

Nicholas was six years younger than me, had three months more sobriety time, was single, and he had roughly rifled through his cousin's pocket and been served a no contact order. When he laughed, he sounded like a cartoon scarecrow.

Over the next four weeks, I listed the ways in which I was powerless over alcohol, but the exercise turned into a grotesque, grand evasion of harsh truths about myself. Working with my new sponsor, Nicholas, had presented new and interesting challenges. He had no wife or children, which I found difficult to relate to, as mine were my whole motivation for recovery. Nicholas commiserated with my views about the exercise. I wasn't interested in excusing my behavior, I wanted to be responsible for myself.

I told Nicholas that Jehovah was my God, but I was beginning to believe it was insane to believe in God. I didn't have the faith to heal myself, and belief in gods felt like delusional thinking. I refused to write down *everything* I was afraid of; instead I focused only on the things I wanted to change about myself or related to my drinking. I made a list of things I resented, people I'd hurt, and determined my part in all of it. I didn't read the list to Jehovah. If He was up there, He knew what I'd written. Nicholas' response to this surprised me.

"Cult status bro," Nicholas said.

I felt validated and empowered by speaking to Nicholas, I began to envision a life outside of Jehovah's Witnesses for me and my family. I was unsure what that would mean in many ways, but I couldn't wait to tell Nova when I saw her and Cyrus the following evening. My visit was scheduled from five to seven. Three minutes before I was due back inside, Nova told me why she'd been acting strange.

"I filed for divorce," Nova said. Her voice was flat, I wondered if she even cared that she was devastating me.

"Why?" I barely exhaled the word.

"If I were someone else, and they stayed with you, I wouldn't respect them." Her tone showed how cauterized she already was. I was in shock.

I missed disassociating. Muscle memory got me back inside Mercy House. I didn't want to talk to Nicholas. I didn't want to talk to anybody except the woman who didn't want to be my wife anymore. Someone threatened to call Jo if I didn't speak to Nicholas, so I agreed.

"This place is filled with criminals, intentional ones," I said. "Surely one of them can help me buy some hardcore drugs I have no tolerance for."

"Why would you want to do that?"

"So I can leave this planet. I do believe I've had enough."

Nicholas sucked his breath and adopted the gingerly tone one uses with the suicidal. "You can't do that. You have a son."

"It didn't work out very well with Ian. Cyrus would be better off with a dead father. I know what I'm talking about." *My dad is dead.*

"You should stick around, you're an asshole. There aren't many left." His soft reproaches normally endeared him to me, but I felt nothing but pain at the moment.

If the situation were reversed, I would tell you to give up. I wish you would lose everyone you love, every belief you ever had and be left among vacuous people you hated. I wished I'd never meet Nova or Ian so I could be spared the agony of losing them.

The next morning the light switch was flipped obnoxiously, and I sat up, squinting.

"Come to the office," Jo said tersely as she walked out the door.

I shuffled down the stairs and flopped into the seat.

"Yeah?" I asked sleepily.

Jo paused with pursed lips and steeped fingers, coolly examining me for a moment, before starting: "Do I need to have the police come pick you up? What made you think you could talk about suicide?"

I furrowed my brow. "I was forced into talking to Nicholas, I was threatened with them calling you and denied being able to sleep which is all I wanted to do. They asked, I told them. My wife just broke my heart."

"She's not your wife anymore!" *That's the whole issue!*

"I thought we were supposed to be honest?" My tone was defiant, but I really couldn't believe I was getting into trouble for expressing sadness at my divorce, at another's request, even.

"That talk is for your therapist. You upset people, addicts are sensitive!"

"Aren't I an addict too? My personal tragedy upset them? Fuck off!"

"Some of them have been up all night checking on you."

"Did you mean the staff being paid? Can you leave me alone? Everyone I love is throwing me away."

"Decisions aren't forever." More cliches.

"Divorce is fairly permanent," I sneered.

"I've been divorced twice."

"So mine doesn't count?"

"You just aren't used to being confronted. You don't like hearing the truth about yourself." Jo had switched from masking her intentions as concern to seeming openly hostile to me now.

"Shut up!" I screamed as I slammed my fist onto Jo's desk. "Shut up or I'll rip your fucking head off!" I'd only yelled for a second, but my chest heaved.

"There," Jo said perfunctorily as she flattened her dress. "You probably feel better now that you screamed."

"I really don't," I said as I opened the door and left the office.

I read my life's history with alcohol to a room full of addicts at Mercy House. Memories had been returning in my sleep, and I wrote them down. I wept as I read about standing over Ian and laughing with a laugh I'd never heard before. The silence in the room reinforced my self-condemnation. I was congratulated for moving into stage two, but I couldn't have cared less. I got my phone back and began researching.

Did I have the disease I kept hearing about, the disease that told me it didn't exist? Was alcohol a sentient, predatory entity, or was I just surrounded by people who shared a victim narrative? Why didn't people speak about how alcohol had addictive properties, or how it increased the release of dopamine and serotonin in the brains "reward center?" People didn't seem to want to admit that alcohol tastes good, or that it's fun to get drunk. Was I denying reality, or were they? Could I not trust myself because my thinking was alcoholic? The more I thought, the more I realized I had little experience thinking. It wasn't exactly that thinking itself was foreign to me, it was more that I had only been allowed to think within certain parameters. I wasn't a newborn – I was a thirty-seven-year-old that jumped from a feigned reality to one I never knew existed.

Jehovah had never removed any of my defects in the past. I didn't expect Jehovah to sort things out, but for the first time I didn't want Him to. I had questions, and even if they couldn't be answered, I wanted to ask them. I was sick of people that lived lives of pretense, fake smiles, and hidden agendas. If I could only stop drinking if Jehovah gave me the power, then what good was that? If Jehovah wanted to intervene in my life, He could have saved my father or kept my mother from rejecting me. I would rather die on my feet as He destroyed me than spend one more second of my life on my knees thanking Him for whatever scraps He gave me.

The presentations I'd given – and sometimes received donations for – targeted the uncertain, afraid, suffering, depressed, lonely, grieving, impoverished and lost. I'd been encouraged to preach in graveyards and write letters to the recently bereaved. I didn't know anybody who became a Jehovah's Witness when their life was going well, including Nova.

While preaching, I told countless people I was a neighbor when I wasn't. I denied that my intention was conversion, but I certainly never led with the most controversial aspects of my faith. I had lied to people.

I was a walking, talking advertisement. I was trained to be articulate, pronounce words properly but not over enunciate, pause, gesture, inflect my voice and use illustrations from boyhood. I was taught to be well-groomed and dressed, honest, cordial, polite, well-spoken, peaceable, loyal, obedient, happy, generous and industrious. I was told to greet newcomers and make them feel welcome. I had love bombed.

I believed that all of the world's problems came from Satan's rebellion and that only Jehovah could fix it all. I believed I could live forever on a paradise Earth, and it didn't matter to me that billions would be killed. We had our own names for many aspects of our faith that outsiders wouldn't understand. We used memorization and thought-terminating clichés. It felt like it was either death at an imminent Armageddon, or blind obedience and denying personal preferences and freedoms in exchange for a chance at the perfect life. I renounced my non-believing family. I had a true "us versus them" mentality and I believed many of my thoughts and desires were sinful. I believed what I believed was more important than anyone else's belief, and that my truth had more authority than the lived experience of any member. I judged, I shunned, and I prayed for the death of billions. Purity was demanded, which led to guilt, confession, and public humiliation. I was judgmental.

I was certain that it wasn't my best thinking that brought me to Mercy House – it was my mistakes. When I was eighteen, my job gave me unlimited access to fried chicken. When I stepped on a scale one day and saw that I was 300 pounds, I knew I wanted to lose weight. I lost over a hundred pounds, so I saw no reason why I didn't possess the determination to never drink again. I knew triggers existed, but they couldn't define my actions. Alcohol is on clothing, in commercials, in entertainment, on billboards and trucks and in businesses. Waitresses don't ask if you want to get started with some heroin.

I told myself I would never accept anything again without scrutinizing it. *Truth like blood waits to get out.*

I texted Nicholas one morning.

I don't believe there is a God.

You can't prove there isn't a God.

I don't have to. Just as I cannot prove there isn't a God, nobody can prove there is a God. It appears we are at an impasse.

Are you sure you're not agnostic?

Yes. If there is a God and you look at what He allows...have you ever heard of dystheism?

What's that?

It's the belief that God isn't good and is potentially malevolent.

What about a doorknob for your higher power?

No. That's offensive. A gorilla is a higher power but that doesn't mean I should entrust my sobriety or life to it. I'm going to smoke before the afternoon meeting.

You smoke now?

Since Nova filed for divorce I've been chain smoking.

You have asthma!

I do what I want.

Dallas was on the porch smoking with three other residents. Bret was a quiet, muscular jock, Carsten was a self-professed pretty boy, and Jadon was a moon-eyed ginger. "Fuck," I thought as I lit a cigar.

"What's up player?" Dallas asked me. *Spare me.* I took a long drag off of my cigar and held the smoke in my lungs, I enjoyed the feeling of rebellion.

"As good as it gets," I said.

"Yo, you're not supposed to inhale those things," Carsten said. "They're bad for you!"

"Truly? What wonderous insight you have. Aren't you a crackhead?"

Dallas said, "Yo dawg, he smoked crack, I smoked meth, you drank. It's all the same."

"I was drinking mouthwash because I figured it was healthier. I drank the yellow," Jadon interjected.

"The fuck dawg?" Dallas laughed good-naturedly.

"Jesus Christ, I don't even gargle with yellow mouthwash," I said.

"You just got to play the game," Dallas said.

"Don't listen to him," I said "What motivates you? It's okay if you want to drink, just because you have a desire doesn't mean you have to act on it. My family, my sons motivate me."

"I wish consequences still mattered to me," Jadon said, defeated. "It's always the same. When I get off of restrictions at my recovery house, I get in my car and leave. Back to sitting under a bridge drinking mouthwash."

"You have willpower. Look man, I don't believe in God but you can do this." *Why am I bothering trying to encourage these guys?*

"When I was a cop, I used to pull people over and steal change out of their cars." Jadon let this statement linger, without any accompanying tone to suggest further internal reflection.

"So all cops are bastards?" I grinned as I attempted to blow a smoke circle.

"There is a God, He's powerful," Dallas interjected.

"This is coming from a flat earther who doesn't believe in gravity but believes in lizard people," I said mockingly.

"You can't prove gravity is real!" Dallas could bellow when he got excited.

I grinned as I dropped my cigar. "What's that? A construct?" Brett snickered.

"Man fuck all that, we got a meeting anyway." Dallas scoffed and went inside.

I told the others, "Never trust a 450 pound meth head. That's like getting fat on broccoli."

"You shouldn't make fun of his weight," Carsten said.

"I used to weigh 300 pounds. I was fat, he is fat. Can we deal in reality?"

"Did you guys smell that?" Jadon asked earnestly.

Carsten asked, "Bro what was that?"

"Dallas," I said. "He hasn't showered in nine days." I lit another cigar. "We've been keeping track."

"You go through those quick!" Carsten said.

"Smoke your cigarette, pussy," I said.

"You're a dick," Carsten said as he lit a cigarette.

"I used to be a nice Christian boy."

"I don't want to be moved into stage two," Jadon exclaimed as he put his head in his hands. He seemed resigned to his dreaded fate.

"I know man, being homeless in a trailer really sucks," Brett said. "Hugging my son will never feel as good as getting high."

"Jesus," I said as I got up.

In the meeting room, Dallas' putrid body odor filled the space. It smelled sweet and sweaty.

Jo announced, "I want you to write down things you may take issue with here at Mercy!"

"To incriminate ourselves?" I asked.

"We don't need any negativity here," Jo said.

"Being pragmatic isn't negative."

"It's anonymous."

"Okay. There are eight people in this room, and my handwriting is distinct, but I'll fill it out," I said snidely. We all shuffled papers and mine went to the person in the room I liked the least: Gus. Gus was in his late fifties, but he looked to be in his seventies. He frequently contradicted himself as he pontificated about the sobriety that ever eluded him.

Gus read my words aloud. "Under 'something I've been struggling with,' they wrote 'being shunned by my mother and friends, going through a divorce, and missing my children.' Under 'something that I don't agree with,' they wrote 'it's asinine that you can't drink energy drinks here. Energy drinks have caffeine in them which is a stimulant so they're bad. Yet we are allowed unlimited soda, coffee, and nicotine, all of which are stimulants!'"

I said, "So that's clearly mine."

Jo leaned against the wall and sighed. She said, "We drink energy drinks because we're addicts, they alter our mental state."

"I drink energy drinks because I'm tired."

Gus chimed in, "Our fucked-up thinking can't fix our fucked-up thinking."

"We know who can!" Dallas said.

"Jesus fucking Christ," I said with a groan.

"Let me speak on this." Dallas said. "Where two or more are gathered, that's what it says. I'm tired of people disrespecting the Lord!" Dallas' skin shined in the light from the window. He continued, "I don't know if anybody around here noticed but I ain't been taking care of myself lately. You know what?" His tone was dejected. Dallas struggled to get out of his chair and stormed out of the room.

"Did we notice?" I asked.

"Do you know what empathy is?" Jo asked.

"To feel the emotions of another person." I answered. "Does he? You practically have to chew through his funk when you walk down the hall."

"Just because something is easy for you doesn't mean it's easy for others."

"Bathing is difficult? He's 40. You'd think with all the God talk he'd know cleanliness is next to godliness. He leaves shit on the back of the toilet."

"Not everyone was taught to not leave shit on the back of the toilet. You have no way of knowing whether or not it was Dallas."

I was flabbergasted. "Don't I? My chore is cleaning the bathrooms and every time I find a wad of shit on the seat it smells like him."

A quiet man with a comb over named Milo suggested, "You know when you're jacking off on the toilet and you scoot back to shoot your nut? Maybe it's from that." He spoke without any shame.

"How about you don't be a filthy motherfucker?" I suggested.

Gus said "You know, it's easy to focus on other people's character defects when we don't want to focus on our own."

"Leaving shit on the toilet is not my character defect." I sneered. "People leave piss on the seat too. My advice is if your dick is too short to aim you should sit like the bitch you are."

"You're not going to stay sober long if you stay angry," Gus said.

After the meeting I tried to call Nicholas to talk to him as I walked to my job, when he didn't answer I left him a message.

That night I discovered Nicholas had relapsed by inhaling compressed air. I wanted to check on him, but I was told I wasn't allowed to. After Nicholas recovered Jo had him tell a room full of men about his relapse. I pitied him as he explained he had quit going to therapy, he'd been starving himself to send his mother money in Oklahoma who was an addict, on probation, HIV positive and suicidal. Finally, I had a chance to see my own problems, severe as they were, in perspective. I apologized to Nicholas if my troubles had been a burden.

"Nah man. Shit, I'm still going to get my one year chip." He smiled a sad, tired smile. "I didn't come to rehab for inhaling compressed air."

"I guess I can try a little heroin then, by that logic. Compressed air, really? You're goofy man."

He chuckled with me. "Still an asshole. Sorry I can't be your sponsor anymore!" Nicholas laughed his scarecrow laugh.

"Don't worry about it, get well," I said.

I didn't want a sponsor, but I knew Jo would insist I had one, so I asked a man named Mickey to sponsor me. Mickey and I were the same age, but like Nicholas, he was unmarried and childless. It was a bad match and I wanted to find someone else, but I worried Jo wouldn't allow it.

"I watch motivational videos daily to keep myself grounded in a positive mindset," Mickey told me. "I have a blog and I do one extra thing each day for my sobriety."

I asked, "On a long enough timeline aren't you fucked?"

"How do you mean?"

"There's only a certain number of hours in a day. Exponential growth isn't realistic."

Mickey blinked. "You take it one day at a time."

"You eat an elephant one bite at a time. Quitting drinking one day at a time maximizes the pain and discomfort of quitting. I quit drinking the day I woke up in jail."

"You think you know everything." I could sense a lot of the same antipathy I felt in Jo in Mickey's responses.

"No. I have questions."

"Questions about what?"

"The Belladonna treatment and its brain-clearing effects for one."

"What about it?"

"Atropa belladonna is a deliriant with the side effects of delirium, hallucinations, light sensitivity, confusion and dry mouth. The second ingredient is another deliriant, hyoscyamus niger, also known as insane root. The third major ingredient is the dried bark or berries of xanthoxylum americanum, which helped with diarrhea and intestinal cramps. The belladonna treatment was given every hour for nearly 50 hours. The end of the treatment was marked by an abundance of stools and was also described as 'puke and purge'."

"What are you trying to prove?"

"How would two deliriants, hallucinations and probably severe dehydration result in a cleared brain?"

"You think too much. Are you afraid to put your faith in something?"

"I'm not afraid. I dedicated my life to God when I was 13, I lived a life of faith. Faith isn't inherently good, it's why people flew planes into the towers."

"You need something to rely on." Mickey's comfort with retreating into the forest of stultifying cliches irked me.

"Why is everyone against self-reliance? I don't believe in God."

"You think there is nothing more powerful than you?"

I sighed. "That isn't a reasonable response. If I was the most powerful entity I sure as shit wouldn't be sitting here talking to you. Did you ever think all of these people relapse because they're praying to the wrong piece of wood?"

"You need a higher power. You have to pray."

"How about my higher power is the half of me that is my father's DNA?"

Mickey paused. "I like that."

"I can't stop drinking myself but if I pray to and rely on that half of myself, that can save me. How is that not delusional thinking?"

"Quit resisting. Have you added to your gratitude list?" Mickey asked.

"No." *If dad was alive, would he even care about me?*

"I noticed you're wearing new shoes. Why aren't they on your gratitude list?"

"Because I have real things on it. I didn't seriously injure Ian. Nova agreed to try couples counseling. The love of my little boy. A thirty-dollar pair of shoes do not belong on a list with them."

"You need to add to it every day."

"Why?"

"Yes, you

"My family is enough."

When an elder invited me to a memorial being held over Zoom, I wanted to wait for nightfall, chug a bottle of alcohol and walk into traffic on the nearby interstate. I told the elder that since none of them cared I was homeless, they could go away forever. The elder robotically responded, "I will go away." I called Mickey and tried to explain how hurt I was, but he cut me off.

"Why do you care?"

"What?"

"They obviously don't care about you. Let it go."

"Am I not supposed to talk to you about my problems?"

"You have stinking thinking. You aren't in the solution." More cliches. Something switched in me.

"I am shunned by my mother and friends, I don't see my wife, I can't talk to Ian and I'm missing out on Cyrus' life." My words tumbled out of me, my tone fire and steel. "My mother will try to get them to join her religion and then they will shun me. Can you even comprehend being erased like that?"

"I've heard all of this before."

"You don't have children, you don't understand."

"File a no contact order against your mother so she can't see your kids."

"I can't, Nova needs her to babysit. I've told her I don't agree but I can't do anything about it. I am a violent felon, a child abuser on probation whose mother filed a no contact against him. No judge will approve that, they will assume it's retaliatory."

"Then stop talking about it." *Simple as. Just stop talking about it.*

I was disgusted. "I'm going back to work."

Mickey sent me a link to a motivational video later in the day and I told him not to do it again because I had real problems. He responded by telling me that I have a victim mentality and asking if I would want to be friends with someone like me. On the walk back to Mercy House I knew I had to tell Jo I needed another sponsor, no matter her reaction. I had an atheist in mind, his name was Liam. I walked into Jo's office and shut the door.

"I need to talk to you about something important," I said.

"Yes?" Jo asked.

"I want to switch sponsors."

"You can't just keep switching sponsors."

"Nicholas relapsed, it's your rule he can't be my sponsor anymore. Mickey is abusive, I already found someone else."

"Someone to co-sign your bullshit? The way I understand it, Mickey offered you a solution and you refused it. You're not in the solution." Talking to Jo and Mickey was like talking to the same half-person.

"He doesn't understand the torture I feel every day, the fear of my mom indoctrinating those boys."

"Oh, it's torture? Are you tortured? You always think you know everything; your mom might not even tell your kids about her religion."

At this point, I really felt myself get heated. What knowledge could she possibly have about that? "She will, she has too. My mother is devout. I need to try to understand what I grew up in, I don't even know what I believe."

"You'll have plenty of time after work and in-between meetings."

"You are not listening to me. I don't know if my mind has been warped by Satan!"

"You think you're so different. I was raised in a cult. There comes a time when you have to decide what you believe in." This stopped me in my tracks.

"I don't know what I believe. Wait...you were in a cult? What cult?" My tone shifted immediately, but Jo's remained firm and distant.

"I don't have to tell you."

I faltered. "You don't, but if you were in one, you'd think you'd tell me about it."

"You think you're so special because you have a bit more education than the people here. I listened to you when you moved into stage two. I know what you are!"

And here it finally was, the root of Jo's dislike of me. Why even bother trying to reconcile, at this point?

I paused for a second, considering my words. "I never used the word special. You're blind and your inability to innovate contributes to relapses. Did you know someone else here grew up like I did?"

"Who?"

"I don't have to tell you! You want to know what's simultaneously best and worst about Mercy House?"

My smirk must have informed her tone, because her "What?" carried an icy edge.

"It's run by addicts."

"Get out of my office."

When Jo called me back to her office Umber sat next to her.

"We have done all that we can for you. It hasn't worked out. You aren't in the solution. I think you just came here so you had somewhere to stay."

"That's why everyone comes here. You let people who relapse stay but you're throwing me out? I'm sober. Liam will be my sponsor."

"You can continue to be sober and Liam can sponsor you, but not here. I called another halfway house called Poornan and they have room for you. It's probably the nicest place you could be other than here."

Deprogramming

An inaudible sigh.
A dulled monotone inflection ebbing into the struggle to find the words I long to convey.
Encapsulated in a vast expanse of knowledge of evil, take another hurried glance.
The banal and the base exalted in their chosen divinity.
A pharmaceutical muse altered to a scapegoat of treason, self-indulgent thoughts parading as reason.
Heaven and hell have lost all demarcation. Shades of gray where I applied bifurcation.
A little Schadenfreude and you're threatening damnation?
A rage stilled for far too long. Illusions to powerlessness and allusions to Gods.
I can't claim to be a hero.
Abounding in pregnant pauses, shadows in the land of the blind.
Hung in a brutal exchange, harsh truths redefined.
When a man lies he lies to himself and God, I am both or I am neither.
Beyond defined, I am divine.

I was a resident of Mercy House for three months, but it was never my home. I contemplated what progress I'd made as I gathered my belongings from a cramped, shared room. My roommate was a crackhead named Devon. He once told me that the first time he smoked crack, he knew why people threw their lives away for it. He also said that he date-raped women because of the disease that he shared with me – the same disease that made us beholden to substances. I told him that he was a rapist and should try owning up to that.

Devon said, "You know, with everything you've gone through...if you gave credit to God for staying sober, they would worship you around here."

"If my sobriety only exists because God gave it to me, then what good is it?" I asked. *I don't need God.* Nova's car slowly pulled up to the side of the curb in front of Mercy House. As I made my last trip to the car from Mercy House, I blithely told Jo "Enjoy your meeting about me!"

Nova was letting me spend the night at her place before taking me to Poornan House in the morning. Ian was staying with his dad. We had some long, difficult conversations on the ride to her place and later that night. She told me that before I had gone to jail, she found evidence of me messaging people online, and that she had asked me to stop drinking. I didn't remember that, but I had no reason not to believe her. I never liked people that cheated, and I had never stopped loving Nova. I confessed to Nova that my drinking and tolerance had gotten to the point where I was blacking out to get drunk, and that I had been drunk almost every day she had known me. She told me she didn't know who I was.

I felt like a monster that had woken up to realize that he'd killed the thing he loved most. That night, as Cyrus slept between us, I reached out and touched Nova's face. She opened her eyes and smiled at me sweetly. I fervently wished the couples counseling would help us. I hated myself for what I had done to my girl.

The following morning, Nova dropped me off at a halfway house for the second time. While Mercy House had never been my home, the constant oversight had provided a mild sense of security and ostensible dedication to sober living. At Poornan House, conversely, the doors did not lock, there was no on-site staff, no curfew, and no sanitation. A preppy douchebag named Trevor told me that I shouldn't care about what I did to Ian, because he wasn't mine. Trevor should have considered that *he* wasn't mine either. Residents regularly stumbled in drunk, and one of them openly smoked crack on the porch while singing 80s pop songs. My room on the third floor had greeted me with dried vomit on the floor and insulation strewn about from the holes in the wall when I moved in.

My recovery – with Liam as my sponsor – continued at Poornan, though I was still attending Mercy House meetings. He once asked me to write a letter to my mother, Jehovah's Witnesses, and myself; to make a list of things I didn't like about myself; and a list of things that annoyed me.

I told Liam, "I'm not making a list of things that annoy me. I'd have to put you asking me to do that on the list."

Liam said, "It won't do any harm."

"There are certain movie endings that annoy me, what relevance does that have to me drinking? I'll do the other stuff." My experience with Jehovah's Witnesses had made me oversensitive to rituals in which I found no utility.

At Mercy House, I read similar letters and lists of things I didn't like about myself aloud in front of Liam before we burnt them. I also read Liam a list of harms I had caused in my life. Nicholas, Mickey and Liam had all heard the list, and the ritual meant less each time I read it to someone.

As I was leaving, I saw Jo and told her that I had ordered a ring while I still lived at Mercy House. I asked her not to return it and to notify me when it arrived.

"Are you sober?" Jo asked.

"Yes," I said indignantly. *That's not even relevant, you stupid –*

As I walked back to Poornan, I called Nova to speak about scheduling our couples' counseling. After we compared work schedules, she told me that Ian had seen the wall hooks and rope I'd ordered on our Amazon account and thought I might come hurt them and tie them up. The actual reason I'd ordered them was to fashion a closet in my tiny room. There was a skylight in my room at Poornan, and I tried to secure a noose from it that night. *Ian deserves not to live in fear, you monster.*

The next morning I awakened to a knock at the door. At the door was one of the downstairs guys who lived at Poornan. He had maintenance workers with him who needed access to the air conditioning unit in my room, so I grabbed my clothes and went to shower. When I came back my wallet was missing from where I kept it on the desk. Despite the small size of the room I inhabited and the walking paths I took at Poornan, I checked them thoroughly, to no avail. When I met Liam to borrow some money from him, he advised me to call the police.

I did file a police report, and when the police showed up Trevor came out to rubberneck. He told the officer that I had left at a different time than I did. I suspected most of the people there were using drugs and wanted them to know I had no issue calling the police to Poornan House. The next day, walking back to Poornan House from work, my phone rang. It was Jonny, another resident.

"Hello," I answered.

"I want to tell you something, you think the world is out to get you but there are good people in it. Someone just gave your wallet to one of the guys."

"Thanks Jonny." *I never once told you the world was out to get me*, I thought.

When I got back to Poornan, Trevor had my wallet.

"Which neighbor turned it in?" I asked.

"I didn't recognize them." Trevor was rather evasive as he handed my wallet back to me.

"Oh, I just had hoped I could thank them. Where was it?"

"In the middle of the street."

"Interesting," I said. I never walked in the street, and my wallet was sopping wet. It hadn't rained in days.

At a house meeting later in the day a housemate was talking about how they were grateful they had found sunglasses they thought they had lost.

Trevor said, "Someone must have stole them!" The group erupted in laughter.

Jonny joined in. "Micah you must be able to relate to that."

"My wallet was found and returned," I said flatly.

"You were quick to assume someone had stolen it."

"It must have fallen out of my pocket," I said with a shrug.

Someone else chimed in, with a sardonic grin, "Alcoholics are quick to blame others."

I nodded. *Of course it's my fucking alcoholic mind.*

Life at Poornan House was essentially life in a room not much bigger than eight by twelve. I left my room only to eat, do laundry or leave for work. I shared cannoli with a mob informant. I was told I couldn't work in a bar and stay sober. I became familiar with Jakob, an unmedicated schizophrenic who told me he heard demons in his room. A few nights later, I saw Trevor whispering under Jakob's door. I told Jakob as much and that he was being pranked, and he locked eyes with me and cautiously asked, "Are you a demon?"

"No," I replied, "but if I was a demon, I wouldn't tell you, would I?"

Jakob's eyes darted left and right. "I guess not," he sullenly replied.

"Please get back on your medication. Think of your daughter."

There were times I wished Jakob would burn Poornan House down and kill everyone in it. One night I heard two grown men, both on house arrest, screaming threats at each other over ketchup. I had to walk 45 minutes to work and back for my bar job and my feet were covered in blisters. I refused to have Cyrus anywhere near Poornan House. I found myself almost savoring the grim irony that people I worked with or met at my job respected that I didn't drink, and the only people that tried to get me to drink were people in recovery.

I called a sober living community called Dorothy Falles and left a pleading message with a woman named Lydia. When Lydia returned my call, I was ecstatic. She ran a background check on me and she told me I could move in, just to give her two weeks. When I talked about being admitted to Dorothy Falles after a meeting at Mercy House, Bud made a face. He was wearing a confederate flag hoodie to match his ring.

"Be careful, I know somebody who relapsed on meth that lived there, so meth is in there."

"There are cocks in Mercy House, be careful you don't suck one," I said as I walked down the porch stairs.

I brought all of my possessions down to the curb early the morning I was to leave, and Nova picked me up. I disappeared from Poornan house without anyone noticing and never looked back.

At Dorothy Falles, I had my own tiny little efficiency apartment with my own bathroom, I had a key to my room, and I could be alone. But most importantly, Cyrus could stay with me. Finally, with a modicum of security in my surroundings, I was able to keep to myself and continue researching my former faith.

I sat outside smoking and ruminating on a crisp evening, when I was disturbed by a woman's voice.

"Are you okay?" she asked with a thick Boston accent.

"I'm fine," I said. *I'm uninterested.*

"Somebody told me fine stands for fucked up, insecure, neurotic and emotional." She had an eager grin, like she was trying to draw me further into the conversation, but it made me even less inclined to engage with her.

"I miss my wife and children." My tone was terse.

"How many children do you have?"

"Two. I'm not happy without them."

"Isn't that just being dry? I didn't get sober to be unhappy. I chose the program because it has such a high success rate."

"Does it?" *What kind of father is happy being estranged from their children?*

"Yes. I'm a recovery coach."

"Of course you are. Look, I am not religious, I am not spiritual. I do not believe you need God to be sober."

"Your higher power can be anything: nature, the sun, a group of drunks."

"It could be, but God with a capital G refers to a creator, and it certainly isn't an acronym."

"Let me give you my number, you call me if you want to hang out." As soon as she was out of sight, I deleted her number.

As I approached one year of sobriety, I reflected back on when I lived at Mercy House, when Liam was almost a year sober. He wouldn't tell people the exact day because he felt like it might somehow jinx things. Superstition had always intrigued me, and I had watched a lot of people be sober for a year and then relapse. I thought that was asinine. Why would I wait a year to drink?

"Why didn't you tell people the exact date when you were approaching a year sober?" I asked him over the phone.

"You can't drink."

I frowned. "It was a question about you, I don't want to drink."

"I don't know that I believe that."

"Name one reason you have to not believe me, name one time I've been dishonest with you."

"I want you to write a letter to your mother."

"Are you out of your fucking mind?" Sometimes it felt like even with Liam, he wasn't listening, we weren't having a real conversation, he too was just that amalgam of phrases and clichés and recovery tropes.

"You have to."

"No, I don't. I'm still on probation and the last time I wrote her a letter her response was a no contact order. I already wrote a letter to her and we burnt it remember? I don't forgive her."

"You have to." No variation in tone.

I was getting irritated. "I don't have to do a God damned thing." Why couldn't anybody just *listen* to me?

"You need to do it for your recovery."

"There are problems without solutions."

"I talked to my dad, Micah. We talked about some dark shit and it got better, Micah."

"My mother believes I serve Satan and is forbidden to speak to me, you have no idea what you're talking about. Stop saying my name."

"I'm not going to stop saying your name, Micah. It makes you stop and listen Micah."

"I'm not your child." His condescension pissed me off.

"You need to stop hating yourself for what happened with your step-son. He sounds like a real piece of shit." That made me livid; Ian was a little boy I loved, even if he *was* a piece of shit, he was *my* piece of shit.

"I just miss having fun." I said. Memories of Nova, Ian and Cyrus flashed in my head.

Liam's voice was glum and heavy. "Me too, I've been thinking about drinking a lot lately." *What the fuck,* I thought, disgustedly.

Nova and I had two therapy sessions before she told me that she wanted to continue with the divorce. She told me when the therapist asked us to consider what we wanted in a partner, she realized she had never asked herself that before. She told me she didn't want to be with me anymore. I collapsed. I had no one to talk to but Liam, so I texted him. I was despairing. Even the effort of talking over the phone would have been like forcing lead from my tongue.

Hope was a waste of time...

What's wrong?

Everything.

I can't help you if you don't talk.

There are no words.

If you don't want to talk why did you text me?

I don't know.

I knew I was being petulant, but I didn't care. Nothing mattered anymore.

That's kinda shitty. I care about you, so talk to me.

No point.

I don't know how to help you when you're being so vague.

Everything is ruined. I need a gun. I can't buy one since I'm a violent felonious individual. I want to die.

No one is going to buy you a gun when you're speaking like this.

I could intuit that Liam was alarmed, but also irritated.

> There is no configuration of words you could say.

> **Why can't you let me help? I've been nothing but supportive! Why aren't I enough? I don't know what to do, especially if you're not going to talk to me. If you don't tell me within 15 minutes I'm done! I can't help you if you don't talk to me.**

The irritation of trying to help the helpless had broken through.

> You can't help me.

> **You have 13 minutes now.**

> Bye.

I was intentionally burning the bridge and I knew it. But I couldn't stop. Part of me wanted to be abandoned, alone, and despondent again. Then there would be nothing to lose.

> **You're throwing people away who just want to help you and not even trying to listen to them and I don't know what to do. Maybe goodbye is for the best. If you actually want to try and work on things**

> then you've got my number. I literally
> don't know how to help or what to do.

I put the phone down.

I told Lydia about my imminent divorce, my lost faith, my estrangement from my children and even Liam, halfway expecting her to discredit my emotions or yell at me. Instead, she validated my emotions and suggested a new sponsor, whose name was David. I found myself liking Lydia very much, she seemed to be one of the few emotionally competent people actually devoted to recovery I'd met in the world of rehabilitation. I went upstairs to my room and called David.

"Hello?" David answered, I recognized his voice. Nicholas had introduced me to him months ago.

"Hi. Do you remember me?"

"I do actually."

"Yeah, we met through Nicholas. I heard he has a girlfriend now which is cool."

"While I do wish him well, when people stop focusing on their sobriety and begin dating it rarely works out. Under every skirt is a slip."

"That's a pessimistic view of things."

"You tend to be pessimistic, but I think you're just tortured."

"I am realistic about my situation."

"Positivity doesn't mean shits and giggles all the time, or maybe it does. Sometimes shit, sometimes giggle. Positivity is sometimes holding on long enough to see the promise of tomorrow, the light at the end of the tunnel."

"Sometimes the light at the end of a tunnel is a train," I said. Cliché for cliché.

"The solution I have found is to ask others what they are doing. Help others. You're in a great position to ask and listen. There are some folks you can help just by listening to their challenges and it will help you!" I was interested in this first conversation. But at the heart of it, I found the same center I'd always come up against.

"I don't want to drink; my reasons and motivations are my own. I am sick of hearing about God. I spent my entire life trying to make others happy or trying to save them. I neglected my wishes and nearly destroyed everything I love. I do believe there is merit in helping others. But right now, I have to focus on myself. I know you don't think I'm open-minded. I want to avoid excuses, rationalizations and relapse. I want nothing to do with faith, God, or spirituality."

David paused thoughtfully. "How do you feel about contempt prior to examination?"

I *was* enjoying this conversation more than the previous ones. "It depends on the context, are we speaking about pedophilia or trying a new food? How do you feel about contempt post examination? Praying to a Higher Power to remove a disease is faith healing. I've heard people say they're trying to fake it until they make it, but when they relapse nobody seems to care. Could it be that they're being set up to fail?"

Another pause. "Interesting perspective, my friend. Thanks for your feedback. I won't break down your words except to say how sad it is you have seen people blamed for relapsing. We shouldn't shoot our wounded."

I appreciated the thought he was giving to my responses. "It is their fault they relapsed."

"They have a disease. Despite their choices once the physical nature of the disease kicks in it takes off like a runaway freight train without any brakes."

Despite the dark fun I was having, I couldn't countenance this line of argument. "If it's a disease, then there must be stages of it. You know Chet? He got his teeth fixed, was facing fifteen years in prison, he just got back visitation privileges with his kids and he decided to be homeless to smoke meth all weekend. I heard somebody normalize that and say regular people wouldn't understand. I'm not claiming to be normal, but that is fucking crazy."

"It was awful to hear about Chet, but it was great to see him celebrate some time." There was genuine sadness in David's voice.

"It was pointless, his children deserve better than to be strung along and think their dad actually was sincere this time. I don't understand."

This is where David regained some confidence in his voice and initiative in the conversation. "Sadly, I do understand, especially as long as I've known Chet. Sometimes we say things are fine when they're not. My biggest downfall was saying things were okay when I wasn't. Sometimes the biggest fear we have is of failing, but fear of success is tricky too."

I chewed on this. "I'm not afraid. I've dealt with my drinking and I am repairing my life."

"Good to hear. Life changed for me when I began sharing what was going on inside of me, surrendered and finally started doing things differently." I appreciated David's humility, but I also knew myself well enough to know that under sharing is not one of my vices.

"I'm kind of notorious for my brutal honesty. I'm tired of people saying one thing and doing the other."

"Do you focus on those who fall off or the ones that soar? Are you always waiting for the hammer to fall?"

"I focus on myself. I'm sick of excuses."

"It only works if you work it, cliché or not. Perspective. Things don't work if you don't believe they won't work. I have a friend who was raised a Jehovah, they went agnostic and then atheist. They've been sober for 18 years. I'll introduce you, I think you two would have good conversations."

I scoffed. "I'll be sober if I'm sober? Delusion, not perspective."

The conversation continued for a while and went well overall. David texted me a few hours after we hung up.

Do you think you played a role in your divorce or not being with your children?

I've never once said what happened wasn't my fault. I've never blamed my family. I've heard people from meetings blame my family though.

Wow, I'm really unsure who you've been talking to. Ninety percent of people blame everybody but themselves until they look in the mirror. Do you have issues with personal relationships or fear?

I do therapy, I don't drink, and I was reflecting on myself and my choices when I was in jail. I drank because my God told me I could drink. These people that get chance after chance and betray their families disgust me.

I've heard people say they'd rather get high then hug their kids, fuck those people. Their children are better off without them. I'm not your strength or here to inspire anyone. I care about my family. I lost fucking everything, my life is over.

Keen observations, interesting indeed. I'm sorry that you feel being sober is a death sentence. Not using mind altering substances like alcohol, drugs, video games, sex and food is just the first part.

I laughed.

How in the fuck am I supposed to not use food?

It's up to the individual. Are you having trouble with personal relationships, emotional natures, depression or money? Do you feel useless? Are you afraid in any way or unhappy? Do you struggle to help others?

Again with the pamphlet treatment. I felt frustrated.

That's vague and essentially describes the human condition. Are you familiar with confirmation bias? I am shunned, I have depression and debt. I'm afraid of sharks. I don't struggle to help others, I don't care. I have to fix my life. I've had depression since my father died.

I appreciate you sharing. I lost my dad and drowned in loss for 25 years. I finally realized self-pity wasn't productive. I was told to get off the pity pot which frustrated me until I listened to their perspective, it changed the way I think. I flipped a switch and now I celebrate his life. I realized I was a victim in many ways and I chose not to volunteer in the past. When I point the finger at someone three more fingers are pointing back at me

It takes a long time to get honest with yourself. I realized when I put alcohol or drugs in me I can't control them. I recognize I'm no different than anybody else on the planet. Your belief that you're different from Chet is interesting. I don't see myself as better or less than, I just pray to be humble. Maybe you'll succeed and maybe you'll fail, I certainly won't judge you or think any less of you. Your terminal uniqueness could be fatal. I wish you nothing but the best and appreciate your honesty.

> If everyone is the same why do you call people
> that can drink without issue "normies?"

David responded 36 days later by saying that he had missed my message because he was camping. He wished me well a second time but I never responded, seeing no point in continuing the conversation. Nearly a year later David texted me again and told me the universe had nudged him to reach out. Spare me.

Mentally Diseased

An awful fulcrum tipped, spilled into dissociative hell.
A displaced persona, sometimes being misplaced is a generosity.
The black hole of realization, a gravitational pull outside of who I was.
Haunted by a reflection on a meditation.
It was and is organic theft. Inevitable victimization. In a countdown, on a timeline.
The mere absence of misery feels like a vice.
I cannot make the egregious claim I love more than I hate.
Spit in His face then you plead? Sweating blood, lost in the need.
The predatory prey while the penitent pray.
Spill what remains.
Emotions numbing, lesions rubbing, legions coming, I'm becoming.
Get the fuck out of my way.

Not long after I met Mickey, Brother Lakstins contacted me. I told him about being mocked by Brother Dunbar and the cover up. His response was "Oh, poo", after which he stopped speaking with me. This man was my father's best friend for years. Later, I saw Brother Rizaldo in a food court. He jerked his head to the side to avoid my gaze. I yelled, "I'd be ashamed to look at me too!" It was as I walked to work one day that I officially became an apostate in my own eyes.

As I walked down the street I saw a Jehovah's Witness next to a cart. *Fuck me*, I thought.
"How are you doing today sir?" The woman's voice was cheery
"Alive," I said flatly.
"Well, that's a blessing, now isn't it?"
"Not really. I hope to be dead soon."

Her smile faltered, replaced with a practiced look of concern. "God doesn't want that for you."

"I don't believe in God."

"Well maybe you can sit down, and we can talk a little about the Bible."

I looked off into the park across the street. "I've read the Bible, many times. I was religious for a long time. The Bible was written by men."

She nodded. "You're partially right, God inspired men to write the Bible."

"I don't believe that, I believe men created God. If there is a God, I do not believe He is good."

"That's where faith comes in."

"Faith isn't inherently good. I was raised what you are. How long have you been a member?"

"Nine years," She said proudly, straightening her head.

"I spent 37 years in your religion."

"Oh, so you already know?"

"I've watched it become something I don't recognize."

She kept the false smile plastered on her face and resorted to proselytization training. "The light keeps getting brighter." *I can't escape from clichés, no matter where I go...*

"Indeed? Are you familiar with the Declaration of Facts, Beth Sarim, or the Australia Royal Commission testimony?"

"No. I'll stick to what I know." Her demeanor notably cooled.

"I know about the mental abuse and mistreatment I personally experienced from numerous elders, and I know about my own mother shunning me when I was homeless."

She demurred. "Sounds like they aren't true Witnesses."

I went on. "I have been privately reproved, publicly reproved, disfellowshipped and reinstated twice, I know your religion."

"You can still return to Jehovah. Only He can judge you."

"Even if you are in the true religion, I will never return. I begged for help and I was rejected, left to live on the streets. Where was your God? I was on my way to work. I hope I didn't upset you or offend you."

"I'll pray for you."

"I bet you will." It was like I was talking to my past self.

Resurrection

As the end of the land is the end of the sea, echoes of you where my heart used to be.
Stale death.
Rigid.
A Frankenstein monster.
"Lazarus rise!"
Frigid.
Rebirth I foster.
Spiritual expiration, visceral frustration.
Entire life was a God damn fiction. Dissonance gone, no mental friction.
No prayer, layers of error and terror.
Voided belief, a vacuum of faith and somber nods.
Avoiding relief, joining the wraith, spare me the odds.
Against all Gods and fuck your facades.

My past doesn't define me, but it is a part of who I am. I know that forgetting the past often leads to repeating your mistakes. When my faith left, it left effortlessly, but the institutionalized guilt did not. After every clap of thunder, I have a moment of panic and wonder if Armageddon has finally arrived. There are times I begin to pray before I eat, a tic I can't quite shake yet and may never lose. I am no longer a religious or spiritual person. I am not dedicated to spreading a message of atheism or lack of belief. I'll certainly never shun in the name of atheism.

On November 19, 2022, I received a letter from my mother after two years of shunning, she asked me to return to Jehovah. If her letter would have come earlier I might have returned to the life I knew. I am an atheist. It's preposterous if my mother believes I don't want to see my dead father again or that I want to prevent their reuniting. My mother told me when I was little I told her I loved her more than all the stars in heaven. That statement is still true but I love my son more than anything.

If I have to choose Jehovah over Cyrus, I say no. I would never shun my son; he is one of two people from my former life who never gave up on me. No matter what mistakes he makes I will support him and never torture him by ignoring him. My love for him isn't obligatory, it is inherent. I do not have the love of God. I would never willingly give up or sacrifice the smallest part of my son. God so loved the world that he gave his son, but I would never choose the world over Cyrus.

I've had people tell me that they pity me because the God they know is one of love, which I believe exposes their delusion. You know God? Does He speak to you? I reject a God who repeatedly commits genocide and then repopulates the world with incest. People with faith have asked me what I think of them, I think they are mistaken. I do not hate people with faith, I do tell them faith is not fundamentally good, many atrocities have been committed in the name of God. I don't need God. I was shackled with faith and being a slave is always a choice, even if it's an ugly choice.

Who is anyone to tell me I can't stop drinking? If you're a fundamentalist, remember that your God said there is nothing men cannot accomplish when the Tower of Babel was being built and He changed languages to stop their progress. Your God seems fickle and insecure. If I had the power to stop all of the suffering on the planet, I know what *I* would do. A good father isn't threatened by the success of his children.

Through the rejection of all that I have ever known – my family, my religion, my support system – I have learned the first *true* thing about myself that I know: I am a man who rejects faith, one who rejects drunkenness, one who seeks to question all presuppositions.

The demarcation between myself and Jehovah's Witnesses has grown since I heard my mother's screams on May 18th, 1996; depression eroded the divide. I've hated myself, cut myself, stabbed myself, burnt myself, broken myself, hit myself in the head until I blacked out, overdosed, hung myself, died, been in a coma, drank myself away, dropped out of college three times, turned down jobs, not asked out women and suppressed my true self. When my half-brother contacted me, I felt guilt over getting to know him and his children because they were worldly. One of my beautiful nieces, Audrey, killed herself before I ever got a chance to meet her. I lost Nova, Ian, Cyrus, my home, my car, and my standing as a law abiding citizen in an instant. I lost my worldview and my hope of eternal life on a paradise Earth. I lost the hope I would hear my father's voice again. I wasted most of my life with people who couldn't have cared less when I was homeless.

A nursing home resident I had taken care of, Janet Lois Raney, told me, "You deserve a life, you deserve a chance." Others told me something similar but I respected Janet and I began to reevaluate my preconceived notions; I started trying to be more understanding. I wondered how to proceed. I refused to be told things about myself I knew were untrue. I once read that people gravitate toward things that are comfortable, even if they're dysfunctional. I came to understand that everything that made me comfortable was unhealthy. I dropped the weight of my faith, belief and shame. I began to look past the narrow walls of my comfort zone.

A woman called me to tell me that I used to contact her in drunken stupors – confirming what Nova had told me. She asked me to "hate-fuck" her, which didn't appeal to me, but I asked if it would be a way of making amends. I didn't bare her any ill will, but I wasn't interested in her. We ended up speaking on the phone and I apologized for hurting her. It was never my intention to hurt anyone but that doesn't matter. I hurt people. I drank away who I was. I hate that my family became my collateral damage most of all. I have a portrait of Ian tattooed on my forearm. I see his six year old face looking at me every day.

I don't need to be a Jehovah's Witness to enjoy life and I don't need to believe in a Higher Power to be sober. I don't believe that recovery from substance abuse is linear, but I reject the proposition that sobriety time doesn't matter. My sobriety matters because when I say I'm going to do something, I do it. I didn't need to let anything go; I needed to analyze, process, and write this book. I am recovered.

I wrote this book to answer that simple four-word question posed by Jenica, who saved my life: "What was it like?" The idea for the book had been gestating, but her question prompted me to set it down as testament to my own journey, as a gift to Cyrus, and as a rejection of self-harm and suicide. My mother wrote her son a letter and I wrote my son a book.

A Letter to "Byrdie"

I love you more than all the stars in heaven. I would never do anything to prevent you from reuniting with my father.

— The boy that you loved, the man that you shun.

A Letter to "Leviathan."

I failed you. I hope that you have healed and that you know you have never been in danger from me since the night I went to jail. In my dreams I see you, standing next to a police officer, looking afraid. I don't remember what your voice sounded like. I have thought of you every single day. Your brother tells me about you and I listen though it breaks my heart. I never wanted to become a monster and if I would have seen it coming I would have stopped it. I knew if I became your step-father there would be times you'd be angry with me, hate me maybe but I never expected things to play out the way they did.

You were one of great joys of my life. I cherished driving in my car with you listening to music. I adored making costumes with you. The concert I took you to was one of the best nights of my life, because I got to share a band I loved with a person I love. I miss cooking with you and playing video games with you. You used to dress like me and that always warmed my heart. You were best man in my wedding.

I'm sorry that I encouraged you to stay away from your family and friends. I thought I was saving you and your mother, I thought I could help you live forever. You were collateral damage during my existential crisis and you never deserved that.

If you hate me I understand and I accept it but I do hope it won't always be that way. I miss you. I love you and I wish you the best.

I hope you are happy "Leviticus."

— M.

A Letter to "Silantius."

I will become an "enemy" of millions for you. I give nicknames to people I'm fond of and you have more than anybody. I keep my watch set to 6:17 P.M. because that is the time you were born. I wanted you from the moment I knew you were growing in your mother. I hope you enjoy life, I hope that you pursue whatever you are most passionate about. I want you to look at the things in the world and know that many of them were built by humans, just like you and I. You are powerful and I hope that you enjoy your life but do not waste your time. Try not to worry what other people think, it's such a waste of time. I want you to question everything, including me. Research both sides of an issue and come to your own decision. If people's words do not match their actions remove them from your life. Do not mistake being polite for being a good person. You don't have to be cruel to accomplish things. Love whomever you want. Know that boundaries are important.

Your daddy may well be crazy. I once sat in a room filled with people who kept talking about how much they loved everybody in the room. I told them I didn't love any of them, love has obligations. I told them I would crush every larynx in that room for you. Maybe I'm crazy or maybe I'm a guy that got sick of being pushed around.

I have worked on this book for over a year and a half, many times while you were in this room with me. I wanted to publish a book since I was a teenager and it will be a dream accomplished to actually hold a copy. It's a really nice idea to think about you reading it one day and knowing me. I will save the first copy for you. I know so very little about my parents. Of all the things I've created you are my favorite. I wish you a great life "Solas."

Mein herz brennt, "Mein Haifisch." I love you.

— Dad.

Afterword

Reality often feels inconsequential. Apostates have been described as "despicable," and "mentally diseased." I would prefer outright hatred to the ambivalence I feel. Can I be hurt by those who shun me when I've shunned others? Can I be angry at people for believing I have joined forces with Satan when I believed that of others? Can I hate people that are encouraged to prove to themselves that they are in the one true religion but can only look at information that is guaranteed to reinforce their beliefs when I obeyed that same caveat? Maybe the only people you're allowed to hate are the ones you truly understand. Truthfully, I pity many of them and miss several.

I realized the impossibility of the situation when I saw a woman I first met when she was six months old. I've adored her since she was that age and her little brother since he was born, I have a tattoo for each of them. Our eyes connected and almost imperceptibly her eyes shifted. She looked in my direction but not at me, she looked through me so thoroughly I questioned my own existence. I felt like I was haunting a life I used to live, I guess I am.

This book began as an explanation fueled by confusion, anger, and regret. I figured one day my son would be curious enough to read it. This is my story but if you have left Jehovah's Witnesses it is your story as well. More than any other reason I wrote this and I accept the oncoming fallout for my son

I hope that you will tell others because children are still being born into the life I've left.
— Micah Allen Losh

Acknowledgments

I used to tell people they could be with me in paradise, this is the best I can do.

Thank you Meena for providing legal counsel.

Thank you Sara for painting who I was and am.

Thank you Moses for helping me tell the story I wanted to tell, whatever becomes of this book it would have been less than that without you.

Thank you to Mica Renee, and Tyler Robbins for taking my author photo.

Thank you to Ali Millar and Natalie Grand for inspiring me to share my story and for encouraging me along the way.

Thank you to the countless EXJWs I interacted with online while I wrote this. Thank you Amber, Alauno, Nika, Mandi, Jesslyn, Stuart, Emmy and so many more. We are legion for we are many.

Thank you Jenica, Daisy, Meredith, Terrance, Tabitha, Mica, Zoie, Bert, John, Paige, Paige, Ana, Moira, Arlie, Eric, Whitney, Maxene, Tyler, Tyler, Jackie, Naomi, Abby, Ayatallah, Julian, Jake, Joe, Joe, Joe, Joe, Brenna, Meta, Amanda, Stone, Bino, Dakota, Andrew, Brandon, Seth, Hunter, Daniel, Connor, Bryce, Elisabeth, PJ, Matt, Zach, Logan, Christian, Aubrey, David, Andrew, Morgan, Chastity, Jereth, Rae, Cam, Caroline, Michelle, Holly, Darrell, Jacob, Emmett, Griselda and any I may have forgotten. You all helped me to realize the world isn't filled with absolute evil. You all live within these pages.

And fuck Greg for trying to make me drink!

Made in the USA
Monee, IL
23 September 2024